Spirituality
for
The Common Man

An empowerment teaching for mankind given through divine guidance from Jesus Christ, featuring The New Beatitudes.

KEITH DAVIS

Copyright © 2011 Keith Davis
All rights reserved.

ISBN: 1456527991
ISBN-13: 9781456527990
LCCN: 2011900435
CreateSpace Independent Publishing Platform
North Charleston, South Carolina
Cover photo courtesy of: www.turnbacktogod.com

Edited by Mary Jeanne Ainsley

Table of Contents

The New Beatitudes Poster xi
Glossary... xiii
Author's Prologue..xvii
Jesus' Dedication..xxv
Jesus' Introduction..xxvii

PART ONE: THE FATHER AND THE SON 1

Chapter 1. You Will Know the Father Through the Son...
Including the New Beatitudes 1-13 3

1. Be God's Will.. 11
2. Be God's Glory 12
3. Be I Am 12
4. Be One 13
5. Be Truth 13
6. Be God's Child 14
7. Be Eternal 15

8. Be Holy 15
9. Be Remembrance 16
10. Be Awakened 16
11. Be an Extension of God 17
12. Be Now 17
13. Be Respectful of All Life 18

Chapter 2. Jesus Is God Personified...Including the New Beatitudes 14-22 19

14. Be Resurrection 21
15. Be the Christ 22
16. Be Authentic 23
17. Be the Golden Rule 23
18. Be Salvation 24
19. Be Renunciation 24
20. Be the Way 25
21. Be the Light 25
22. Be the Atonement 26

Chapter 3. My Intentions Are Love and Forgiveness... Including the New Beatitudes 23-31 27

23. Be Love 32
24. Be Loved by God 32
25. Be Love for God 33
26. Be Loved by Me 33
27. Be Love for Yourself 33
28. Be Love for One Another 34
29. Be the One Mind 34
30. Be the Miracle 35
31. Be Joy 36

Chapter 4. Why Forgiveness Is a Part of Me...Including the New Beatitudes 32-40 37

32. Be Innocent 44
33. Be Forgiveness 44
34. Be Directed by the Holy Spirit 45
35. Be Non-Judgment 46
36. Be Acceptance 46
37. Be Compassion 47
38. Be Tolerance 47
39. Be Defenseless 48
40. Be Healed 48

PART TWO: YOU WILL SEE WITH MY EYES 51

Chapter 5. If You Love and Forgive...Including the New Beatitudes 41-49 53

41. Be Vigilant 58
42. Be Whole 58
43. Be Equal 59
44. Be Free 59
45. Be Faith 60
46. Be Detached 61
47. Be Transformed 61
48. Be Discipline 62
49. Be Peace 62

Chapter 6. You Are Already Deserving...Including the New Beatitudes 50-57 65

50. Be Already Deserving 67
51. Be Guided 67

52. Be Infinite 68
53. Be Beauty 68
54. Be Confident 69
55. Be Wisdom 69
56. Be Balance 70
57. Be Hope 71

Chapter 7. Why You Will See With My Eyes...Including the New Beatitudes 58-66 73

58. Be Responsible 78
59. Be Aware 78
60. Be Aligned 79
61. Be Intentional Creation 80
62. Be Present 81
63. Be Intentional Breath 81
64. Be Intentional Thought 81
65. Be Intentional Choice 82
66. Be Practice 83

Chapter 8. What You Will See With My Eyes...Including the New Beatitudes 67-73 85

67. Be Trust 87
68. Be Intuition 88
69. Be Integrity 88
70. Be Understanding 89
71. Be Passion 89
72. Be Imagination 90
73. Be in the World but not of the World 91

PART THREE: MAKE THIS LIFETIME COUNT 93

Chapter 9. How to Achieve Closeness to Me... Including the New Beatitudes 74-81 95

74. Be Surrender 100
75. Be Willing 100
76. Be Humble 101
77. Be Service 101
78. Be Sharing 102
79. Be Prayerful 103
80. Be Abiding 103
81. Be Simple 104

Chapter 10. Why Achieve Closeness to Me...Including the New Beatitudes 82-89 105

82. Be Well-Being 109
83. Be Blessed 110
84. Be Endurance 110
85. Be Enthusiasm 111
86. Be Safe 112
87. Be Restored 112
88. Be Sustained 112
89. Be a Channel 113

Chapter 11. What Happens If You Achieve Closeness to Me...Including the New Beatitudes 90-98 115

90. Be Empowered 120
91. Be Courage 121
92. Be Victory 122

93. Be a Teacher 122
94. Be Allowing 122
95. Be Strength 123
96. Be Enlightened 124
97. Be Sacrifice 124
98. Be Heaven on Earth 125

PART FOUR: GRACE AND GRATITUDE 127

Chapter 12. Be Grace...Including the New Beatitudes 99-106 129

99. Be Grace 130
100. Be Mercy 131
101. Be Patient 131
102. Be Honest 132
103. Be Just 132
104. Be Gentle 132
105. Be Self-Control 133
106. Be Still 133

Chapter 13. Be Gratitude...Including the New Beatitudes 107-114 135

107. Be Gratitude 138
108. Be Generous 138
109. Be Open-Minded 139
110. Be a Friend 139
111. Be Abundant 140
112. Be Order 141
113. Be the Kingdom of God. 141
114. Be Ascension. 142

Appendix
The New Beatitudes 147
The New Beatitudes "I Am" Statements of Being 151
A Memoriam to Harvey Carter Lane, Jr. Be Eternal
Dad's NDE 157
About the Author 161
Appendix 163

The New Beatitudes
Poster.

Visit www.spiritualityforthecommonman.com and subscribe to download The New Beatitudes poster. This is a professional artist's design listing The New Beatitudes in a beautiful format suitable for framing. You can also check out the 114 New Beatitude videos Keith filmed to clarify each one, as well as our latest news, weekly meditation thought, newsletter, products, services, blog, study groups, and upcoming webinar program.

Thank you for your interest in The New Beatitudes and your contributing love, forgiveness, and Oneness for all creation. Together we can change the world for the better and inspire mankind to *be love* and *be forgiveness now.*

Go to: http://spiritualityforthecommonman.com

Glossary

The following words, phrases, and meanings are important for a true understanding of Jesus' message:

All That is: The Father, The Son, and The Holy Spirit or the Holy Trinity.
Be: To *be* (italicized for easy recognition) is to believe in your divinity, express it, and do it now; it is *being love, being forgiveness,* and being The New Beatitudes as your divine Self.
Christ: The divinity and potential for perfection that represents God's nature and character within all; Christ will always *be love, be forgiveness,* and *be One*.
Christ Temple: Being the embodiment of Christ consistently by being human and divine with no separation or gap between the two.
Ego: Your limited, physical self and mind that thinks only of itself and believes in fear, separation, death, and illusion.

God's Child: Child is capitalized since the Father's creations are holy extensions of Him and One within Him.

Holy Instant: Asking the Holy Spirit to direct you in *being forgiveness* and being your divine Self, where you reside in peace beyond the world by letting go of your personal identity.

Holy Spirit: God's voice for Truth and your internal guide who heals your separated mind and directs you in *being forgiveness* unconditionally.

I Am: The Father is I Am that I Am, and being an extension of Him, so are you.

Innocence: The Father's energy, presence, and love that is within all life as One.

Innocents: Babies, animals, and nature are those in a state of innocence; they are teachers of unconditional love and forgiveness and must be respected.

Mind: The capitalized Mind is the universal intelligence and higher power of the Father, as opposed to the physical mind.

One: Or Oneness is capitalized, being of the Father or One, and divinely interconnected with all life as One. There is no separation or division in the One or God' creations.

Self: With a capital "S" is the divinity within all life that is of the Father; it is the soul and Higher Self or power that is innocence, love, Truth, Oneness, joy, peace, and eternal.

Soul: The higher Self that is what God is, I Am, and you are.

Spirit: The life force and energy body of a soul.

The Common Cause for the Common Man: *Being God's Will* is being the common cause for the common man. God's Will is Truth, Oneness, innocence, love, peace and joy for all.

The New Beatitudes: Jesus Christ's empowerment teaching for mankind, consisting of 114 italicized phrases (within this book) that are keys to spirituality and attitudes of Mind that guide you in the way to *be*, thus they are *be* attitudes.

Thought: The capitalized Thought is of the Father, *being Truth, being holy, being innocent, being loving,* and being the New Beatitudes in all ways.

Truth: The Father's Will, Thought, vibration, and energy.

Author's Prologue

Jesus has asked me to speak about my spirituality and our journey together writing this book, so you will understand that the same closeness I enjoy with Him is possible for you, if you so desire.

Writing this book through divine guidance from Jesus Christ has been quite an extraordinary experience, spanning the last five years of my life. These teachings have healed my soul and changed my perspective in many wonderful ways, and they reflect how I live my life now.

They have also expanded my awareness of the real nature of mankind beyond my limited beliefs. The New Beatitudes include the grandest truths I could ever imagine and the greatest message in the world. In fact, Jesus' message is out of this world, as you will see.

Jesus has taught me to remember that I am not who I have believed myself to be. Now I understand my Self to *be God's Child* and an extension of the Father's being, Will, glory, nature, and character. We are all God's beloved One Son, whose reality is so great that what you previously thought about yourself pales in comparison to your authentic Self, which is who you really are.

Our egos have convinced us to think less of ourselves, and to believe in the illusive ways of the world. But Jesus asks us to see through His eyes, beholding ourselves as we truly are in holy vision.

As you are awakened to see things differently, you will realize that you already are these New Beatitudes. All you might do is change your mind and be who and what you are meant to *be*. Then you will *be* these New Beatitudes now as your "Self." Your Self is the part of you that is aware of your divinity, so it is written with a capital "S," as compared to yourself that is unaware of God within you.

Even more, being your Self you will *be the Christ* temple, or embodiment of Spirit. *Being God's Will* and *being an extension of God* as His beloved Child, you are One with Him, within Him, and He is within you as well. *Being One* is a key to life that realizes only unity and interconnection between all living beings; so there is no disconnection or separation ever. Incidentally, the keys at the bottom of the pages represent the keys to life or *be* attitudes, that are definitely the way to *be*.

Therefore, you are Spirit in a physical body having a human experience, being very capable of communicating with, listening to, and *being guided* by God, Jesus, and the Holy Spirit, as One and *being One*. You may also *be directed by the Holy Spirit* whenever you ask.

Welcoming the Holy Spirit to direct your mind and teach you how to *be unconditional forgiveness,* you will *be,* which is being The New Beatitudes as your divine, higher Self. The more you surrender, ask, pray, and receive guidance, the easier it is.

Surely, no matter what religion you are, or what you choose to believe or not, *being love* and *being forgiveness* are the ways to change your life for the better now. They are also the ways to be the change that is so deeply desired in the world today.

Thus, my spiritual journey began as a small child, when my dear mother and grandmother, Mamaw, taught me to love God, trust Him, and be grounded in the certainty of my belief. I have always had a special place in my heart for Jesus as well, naturally feeling very connected to Him. I have always been God's girl and proud of it, even when I was teased about it. And now, after this intensive work with Jesus writing the book, I refer to myself as Jesus' girl.

My beloved mothers also instilled within me the surety and foundation of God's love, protection, and grace no matter what came my way. They taught me that God created me and I belonged to Him as well, so I always have known whose I Am. And I am grateful since my spiritual beliefs sustained me throughout the worst trials of my life, empowered me to overcome depression and addiction, healed my aching heart, restored my joy and self-esteem, enabled me to walk through the dark unafraid, and inspired me to always be my best.

Certainly, life is not easy and we learn many of our greatest lessons through strife. Like many of you I have experienced much hardship and pain. When I was eight years old and much to my great dismay, my mother died and my world was turned upside down. After my mother's death I continually searched for her and her whereabouts, desiring to know more.

My mother was in Heaven; yet could she still communicate with me? Would I ever see her again and was she watching over me and helping me in my life? Was she with God, Jesus, our departed family members and beloved pets, and would we all be reunited in Heaven in eternal life?

These questions and more prompted me to continue my search for knowledge of the other side and the truth of life. Incidentally, the answer to all of these questions is an enthusiastic "yes."

I have been further surprised to realize that I am clairaudient, which is the ability to hear the unspoken; consequently, I can communicate with my loved ones in Heaven through divine guidance. For decades I have heard messages from my dear departed mother and grandmother, and my spiritual guides. In 2005 my dear friend, Sharon Day, who has been divinely guided by Jesus Christ all her life, miraculously brought Jesus in for me.

During a healing session with Sharon and much to my astonishment, Jesus appeared before us. In this life changing moment, Jesus comforted, healed, and guided me in the way to *be*. He also asked me to write a book with Him through divine guidance, and I told him I would try.

I asked Jesus how I would know his voice and he told me to journal 100 pages with him. This took three months and throughout the process I learned to recognize his profound, beautiful voice. Even now, whenever I call on Jesus, he is always there, responding in words, pictures, or visions that convey his answers and thoughts, and I am so grateful.

Finally, after working with Jesus for five years and writing over eight hundred pages, we edited the manuscript to approximately a hundred or so pages and *Spirituality for The Common Man* was born.

Writing this book and giving mankind The New Beatitudes is my mission in life. It is also the reason I am here now, combined with my desire to be the best mom ever. Truly, Jesus is the sustaining force of my life, because He is everything I desire and my closest friend.

I know for sure that the principles in this book are a Godsend, since I have always felt guilty and sinful, thinking that God was angry with me for my sin, as my Methodist religion taught. But, now I know a better way; now I know the way.

My perceptions were just that, opinions and beliefs that I thought were true, but they were not God's Truth. I now know that God's Truth is better than I ever imagined, since it is our Truth as well. I have learned that we can change our minds and lives with new choices to *be*, by seeing with a new perspective through Jesus' eyes in holy vision.

Being these New Beatitudes my Self, I desire to always *be love* without grievances and *be forgiveness* automatically, rather than to judge automatically. I also ask the Holy Spirit to direct my mind in *being unconditional forgiveness* every day. Whenever any negativity flares up, He heals my mind and corrects my thinking, allowing me to truly *be forgiveness*.

If you can wrap your head around these teachings, you will be close to Jesus and fulfill your soul's purpose. If you find that personal change is called for, you are the one to choose it and *be* it, because you are responsible for your own healing.

Besides being the best that I can *be*, there is nothing I desire more than for Jesus' will to be my will. My life is His life, since I live to serve and glorify Him by being these New Beatitudes my Self, and inspiring mankind to *be* them too. I also desire to shift the collective consciousness of the planet from fear to love, joy, peace, enlightenment, and ascension now.

Even more, I especially hope that this teaching awakens mankind to the reality of One soul and the sacredness of all life. I know for sure that it is very important to respect and care for the Innocents, who are babies, animals, and nature. A human's relationship with the Innocents directly reflects the soul's relationship with the Father,[1] so *be One, be respectful of all life,* and *be service* for others before yourself.

Furthermore, Jesus has said that he will give a miracle to everyone who reads, holds, or even looks at this book. This means that he will come in personally so you feel His Presence and see His hand in your life in a very real way. Certainly, I look forward to your experience of Jesus and the resultant miracles that follow.

For those who are interested in my personal, fully developed story you can check it out in my upcoming book, *Why I Am Chosen*. But for now, I will say that in this life I have found our deepest pain gives us unexpected gifts. I am sure that the searing pain I've experienced has prepared me for this teaching.

Spirit has shown me that there is a soul group of many great souls who chose to bring in the New Beatitudes. I have been shown a vision of us gathered around Jesus and many other masters. Jesus asked the group who would be the messenger for the teaching, and after an awkward silence I raised my hand and said, "I will serve my Lord."

Then it was decided that I would be seared in pain so deeply that I would depend totally upon Jesus and God. The plan was for me to experience childhood abuse and abandonment by my father. Additionally, my mother, infant son, three other embryonic children, and grandmothers

---

[1] Sharon Pieroni Day, The Book, The Creator's Template for Eternal Life, (Create Space, Charleston, SC, 2010) p 113

and grandfathers would die or transition, my marriages would crumble, and consequently my elderly father whom I cared for, my oldest son, and I would be taken in by my beloved brother. Hardships would continue but I would rise victorious through adversity by being the strength of Christ.

Now, walking my talk and being the living personification of this teaching is my goal and daily task. Many times I remind myself that many family members died for this cause so I can certainly do what I agreed to do. In *being God's Will* and being dominion over the world, by *being in the world but not of the world*, I know myself to *be God's glory!* Being let down by those whom I depended upon, I have learned that I can depend on my Heavenly Father and Jesus completely, that they have never hurt me, and they never will.

Certainly, I am 100% responsible for my life and the choices I've made. Yet, I gladly forgive myself and all those concerned, and I gratefully appreciate the resultant life lessons and character building training that has molded me into the pillar of strength, faith, and humility that I have become.

Additionally, I acknowledge eternal life through my father's recent near death experience, which confirms the belief in life after death, and this will comfort many people. Through my gifts of divine guidance and healing, I gladly support those in the throes of despair and sickness by sharing Jesus personally with them.

I will rest when my mission is accomplished, and mankind has shifted into the highest dimensions of love, joy, healing, peace, and enlightenment. Love is the way, forgiveness is the key, light is the touchstone, and joy is the purpose that inspires us all to dare greatly and *be now*.

Finally, I dedicate this book to Jesus in deep appreciation for gifting me with this heartfelt mission, and for the infinite joy of the journey.

I would like to share one of my daily prayers with you now, which is: "Father, Jesus, Holy Spirit, and Blessed Mother, my will is your will, my life is your life, how may I serve you today?" Then I go about my day *being prayerful* and being a prayer, which is being so continuously connected to Spirit in every thought, word, action, and feeling that my life is a prayer. I trust all, surrender all, love all, forgive all, and allow all, *being gratitude* for all that is, being I Am that, I Am.

With all my heart, I am deeply grateful to my beloved family, friends, and support team here and on the other side, for having my back. Thank you all for believing in me and the love that we share.

Thus, I stand in grace and gratitude for the opportunity to share this teaching with mankind. And as Jesus has asked, I desire to further the common cause for the common man by inspiring mankind to *be God's Will now*. So *be* it!

Always *being love* and *being forgiveness*,
Keith Davis

Beloved One, I dedicate this book to
every common man and woman of the Earth.
Each of you are Spirit within a physical body
having a human experience.
You are playing the game of life in order to understand
your true identity, which is love,
and your true purpose, which is to *be love*.
You have chosen the Earth plane
in which to expand love, practice forgiveness,
explore contrast, and express your divinity
so as to evolve and reside in a higher realm of Heaven.
Being the Christ temple, Mind, and consciousness is
unifying the human self and the divine Self in One body,
and this is what The New Beatitudes inspire you to *be*.
The joyous interconnection of yourself
and All that is, *being One* within the One,
is the intention of your birth and
the spiritual manifesto of a life well lived.
And so may you *be*.

JESUS CHRIST

Jesus' Introduction

I rose from the dead and so can you. My resurrection demonstrated eternal life and yours can give you new life now. *Being resurrection,* you can leave the ashes of your fearful past behind and release all that no longer serves you. By awakening and seeing things differently with a new perspective, and changing your mind about reality, you can become the most loving version of yourself possible, and be who you are meant to *be.* You can become a divine human, and be divinely human, or more simply said, be divine. And that is what this book is all about.

Over two thousand years ago in my lifetime as Jesus Christ I gave mankind The Beatitudes. They are my original teaching about how one might live a blessed life in accordance with God. You will find them recorded in the Scriptures of the Holy Bible in Matthew, Chapter 5, verses 3-11, as follows:

Blessed are the poor in spirit, for theirs is the Kingdom of Heaven.
Blessed are those who mourn, for they shall be comforted.
Blessed are the meek, for they shall inherit the earth.
Blessed are those who hunger and thirst after righteousness, for they shall be filled.
Blessed are the merciful, for they shall obtain mercy.
Blessed are the pure in heart, for they shall see God.
Blessed are the peacemakers, for they shall be called the children of God.
Blessed are those who are persecuted for righteousness sake, for theirs is the Kingdom of Heaven.
Blessed are you, when men shall revile you and persecute you and say evil against you falsely, for my sake.

Now, I answer your calls for understanding and enlightenment, by offering my gift of The New Beatitudes to every common man and woman. They are attitudes of Mind that guide you in the way to *be*, and thus they are *be* attitudes.

Verily, The New Beatitudes are keys to spirituality and empowerments for being that reveal the Truth of life. Each one is a Self-fulfilling prophecy that unlocks your ability to be Self-realized by inspiring you to change your limited perceptions and be who you are meant to *be*.

Through them you will realize who you are, what you are, and why you are here now. Each New Beatitude will open your mind to the divine Intelligence that you are, while empowering you to be your greatest potential and create your best life now.

Even more, these New Beatitudes will guide you in the way to see things differently. They will encourage you to change your perspective from fear to love, so you find your way back to the Father as One.

You will further realize that your life is formed by your beliefs, thoughts, words, actions, and feelings, rather than by your own personal circumstances. Limited conditions in the world can change instantly, being overcome by God's Will, God's glory, Truth, Oneness, love, forgiveness, peace, joy, and gratitude. Therefore, you may be all that you desire to *be now*, being unlimited in your ability to *be*.

Most assuredly, these New Beatitudes direct you in the way to make this lifetime count. For, as you embrace this journey that is all about your soul's evolution, your real identity, your true purpose, the illusion of the world, the innocence of all living beings, your intentional creations, your relationships with God and me, your relationships with others, and the importance of grace and gratitude, you will see with my eyes in holy vision.

Applying these principles, you realize what you accept in your mind is manifested in your life. You must *be willing* to observe your fears, judgments, and the past so you may forgive them and choose love. Then you can realize your Self *being One* with Spirit, as Spirit, with no separation between the two. Believing and acknowledging your divine Self to *be an extension of God*, you will think, speak, and act accordingly, *being I Am* as your Self, or being divinely human.

This new way of thinking asks you to *be willing* to shift your paradigm from a human or physical reality to a Spiritual, non-physical reality. And thus you merge yourself with your Self by seeing things differently, *being aware* of your soul's magnificence, *being acceptance* of the extension of God that you are, and being it now. This is fulfilling your soul's divine purpose, and the Father's intention and plan for His beloved Children.

Then you intentionally choose to *be* each New Beatitude so fully, that you become the aspect your Self. For example, you may *be loving* in every thought, word, action, and feeling so often and continuously that you become love, and finally *be love*. You may also *be* more love by giving away these aspects of love continually, and thus increase the experience, expression, and expansion of each one. And thus you will *be* The New Beatitudes your Self and inspire and elevate others to *be* too.

Being practice, becoming, and being The New Beatitudes your Self contributes to the enlightenment of humanity and well-being of all life. Acknowledging them as your Truth and being them in every thought, word, action, and feeling is very worthwhile. Since all Minds are joined, you can make a difference and be the change that heals the world by *being the light* and *being the miracle* that constantly shines love, forgiveness, and Oneness unto all.

Surely, there is a better way than the world's way of being, and I am here to *be the way*, the Truth, and the life now. Thus you are being called upon to *be the Christ* with your name, your Mind and heart, your own thoughts, words, actions, and feelings, and your own hands and feet.

Recognizing that you actually are the divine Mind of God, or Christ Mind, you will see things anew. Gone are your limited, little beliefs of fear, negativity, judgment, guilt and shame. For surely you are divine Oneness, life, intelligence, power, and awareness. Thus, you are perfect, holy, worthy, innocent, beautiful, and whole now! Your only shortcoming may be your mistaken identity, and that can be changed in an instant as you understand your divine truth and *be Truth*. This revelation in itself is an awakening, remembrance, healing, transformation, and resurrection of your Self and invitation to *be now*.

With your divinity established, it is possible to understand that a place where God dwells is a temple. So all life, all the earth, all places, all people, all animals, all words, all interactions, and all things are temples where God lives. He is everywhere and everything is holy. All life is Spiritual and sacred, all things matter, and everything is connected and divine.

God lives within you as the holy Christ temple, or the embodiment of potential perfection. With your beliefs, thoughts, and choices *being aligned* with God's, you may live a spiritual life, being Spirit yet human. Not only can you live a spiritual life, you are spiritual life manifesting as I Am, so *be I Am*. *Being I Am* you may exit illusion and be divine Spirit by remembering your true identity and being it now.

Even more, all life, creations, and beings are sacred because God lives there. The human and divine live within the One Mind and body, so all Minds and matter are infused with God's energy and life, *being One*. Further, there is only One soul that is God and the One divine Self. There is no separation in God's creation, being All that is, as God in All as All, and I Am that I Am, so *be I Am* and *be One now*.

Since God lives within your Self, mind, body, and temple, it is good to *be aware* of your holiness and creations. *Being an extension of God* you have the power to bring about a shift in the collective consciousness from fear to love, from judgment to forgiveness, from conflict to peace, from sickness to healing, from suffering to joy, and from limitation to magnitude.

In my lifetime as Jesus Christ I embodied God while being human, and thus I was divine and human within one body. Your task is the realization of the Christ with your name, being the presence of God your Self, and this is your soul's true purpose. By my example, the Christ pattern for perfection is your true identity and what I am inspiring you to *be now* as I Am.

Even more, Christ is the name for the realization of this elevated awareness that is possible for everyone. Since all human beings are extensions of the Father as His beloved Children, they possess the God Mind or Christ consciousness. Whether they choose to access it and *be* it is an individual choice, but everyone has it. Thus, it is the state of mastery that many great teachers such as Mohammed, Buddha, Dalai Lama, Rumi, and I attained, and that you may *be* also with every intentional choice to *be love now.*

So as you can see, Christ is not my last name nor is it exclusively mine! But it is the name for all who personify the glory and goodness of the Father as their divine Selves, *being the Christ* with their names. Surely, there are no imperfections within God's creations, only limited awareness of who you are and meant to *be.* For great are the riches and glory of Christ in you as your infinite Self.

Being the template of perfection as the Christ with your name, you may actualize your true identity, which is unconditional love, and your true purpose which is to *be love.* Being Spirit within a physical body having a human experience, you may also choose to *be love for God* and His creations. Your Christ Self or internal being is an extension of the Father, who is your Creator and the power that created all things. So it is good to love Him and allow that love to prevail throughout your life. *Being love for God* opens your heart and One Mind to the love that you are, and the infinite vastness and capabilities of your divine Self.

If this is not your choice or perspective, you will love yourself or physical self first, and the external things of the world. Control and power will be your prevailing intentions; regard for personal fulfillment and the outer self dominate your perspective, attitudes, and actions.

If your outer love continues unchanged, you will be limited by worldly constructs and negativity that enslave and inhibit your freedom to *be*. There will never be enough things to fill your appetite for power and control, because the insatiable ego always hungers for more.

Surely, the Father has planted a part of Him Self within you which is your divine Self, soul, or higher power. If you acknowledge your divinity and allow an awareness of it to expand and evolve, you will be close to God and me. If you don't love God, and develop a relationship with Him, there will always be something missing, which is your prevailing love for your Father whom you are an extension of and within, *being I Am*.

Understanding your love for God predicts your intentions and actions, and how you feel about life. It also foretells your basic character, purpose and motivations. It outlines your nature as well, while determining how you feel most often and why.

All in all, it comes down to a choice between inner Self or outer self, divine Self or yourself, self-love or love for God, and fulfilling your soul's purpose or something else. Another words, you can either *be love* or fear and the Father desires for you *to be the One Mind, be intentional thought,* and *be intentional choice* to *be love for God* and His creations, *be the light, be a blessing, be a healer*, and *be the miracle* worker now.

More cause for contemplation is the question you will be asked upon your arrival in Heaven after this lifetime, which is, "How well did you love?" Howbeit, did you love yourself, power and control, and the things of the world the most? Or were you motivated by a prevailing love for God and His creations?

Being love for God, did you love all others as your Self, did you respect all life, did you hold anything sacred, did you honor your relationships, respect your elders, consider all equal, tell the truth, forgive all, strive for excellence, find joy in the moment, appreciate all, bless all, serve a cause higher than yourself, and exemplify the Christ as your Self?

If you loved well, then God bless you, beloved. If not, then God bless you too, as you receive another opportunity to love well and express, expand, experience, and evolve as love personified. Either way, you will feel how you made others feel in your life review, and this will either *be Heaven on Earth* or something less. In any case, this picture is cause for reflection, evaluation, and improvement as you consider how well you loved.

Furthermore, *being Heaven on Earth* you will intentionally choose to *be love for God* and belong to Him, by *being God's Child*. Being mutually loved and loving, your will appreciate your relationship with the Father that respects, honors, supports, and inspires the beloved to be loved more, become more loving, and *be love now.*

As you can see, *being the Christ* with your name is your divine purpose and destiny, the gift of a lifetime, and my blessing upon you now. As you acknowledge the Father and the Christ that you are, you will be the presence, nature, and visible likeness of God as I Am.

Furthermore, the evolution of mankind will shift as these universal empowerments for being are realized, and salvation will come unto everyone by their own love and forgiveness.

Dear One, you are my beloved, and I will always be with you. I will never leave you or forsake you, for you are within me as my Self.

Thus, I desire for the common man to be united in a common cause: *be God's Will now.* So *be* it!

JESUS CHRIST

Part One

THE FATHER AND THE SON

Chapter 1

You Will Know the Father Through the Son

This world needs me. Too many people are burdened with pain and hardship, and sickness abounds. Religions are teaching fear and damnation in hell, with little hope and certainty for the future. Natural disasters and uncertain economic times are forcing more and more people into poverty. Political unrest is ongoing and Mother Earth is being disrespected in the name of progress. People are lost and misguided and killing one another in God's name and this cannot be.

It is time for the prodigal Son to turn toward the Father instead of away from Him. It is time to be as a little child and depend on the Father, so you may truly *be empowered* as His beloved. It is time to open your heart and renew your faith. It is time to change your mind and see things differently. It is time for love and forgiveness to save the day, because they are the only things that can!

I am here with you now as Jesus Christ of Nazareth, and, yes I am alive today. I only died physically as everyone eventually does, but my Spirit has lived on and I have been with you always. I have come forth now because you have called me, and I have heard your every thought and word.

In response to your calls for help and guidance, I give these keys of life to every common man and woman. They are everyone's reality, regardless of your religious beliefs or absence thereof. Therefore, you may embrace them or ignore them, but they will always *be Truth.*

Verily I say, it is time for humanity to come unto me and rejoice, for I have overcome the world, and so can you! The good news is that the answers to life are not in the world, but within you as your divine, true, higher Self. Your Self is written with a capital "S," because it is divine, rather than yourself which is of the ego and the world.

Through these New Beatitudes, you will realize that you are an extension of the divine Self of the Father or God. The Father is All, All That Is, I Am that I Am, One, the Infinite Intelligence, eternal Spirit, and power of Creation, being life and love It Self. The Father or Abba, is also your Father who loves you unconditionally and devotedly in all ways and beyond all time.

I have said, "The Kingdom of God is within you"[2] and it certainly is. Your Father only creates like Him Self, so you must be God's Son. I am the Son who chose to be an

---

2 Luke 17:21

example of the Father. It is through me that you know your Father and who you may *be* as God personified.

I have said that God has only One Son[3] who is all of us. Yet, now I add that every common man and woman is God's One Son, because His Children are One creation, even if they are Sons or Daughters, because All is One and there is no separation in the One. So *be One* and *be the Christ* Self or One Self that is God's Self, the Holy Spirit, and my Self. Through the Father's grace and extension, the innocence and love of God's Self is also in every being that lives and breathes.

Herein is the Truth of Being that you are. Being within your Father as His One Son, you are blessed to be His beloved Child. The "beloved" is the unconditionally loved and loving Self of you that is God, and this is why I call you beloved.

Being God's Child you are One of the One, because there is no separation[4] in the One. All is One, *being One* Spirit, One soul, and One life. God is the only power, being the Creator of All life and All things; so you cannot be separate from the Father's love or your real Self. Any division is only your perception and not real.

Therefore, you may embrace the vast unconditional Oneness that you are by *being One* now. In so being, you will do unto others as you would God and your Self. You will also acknowledge, accept, and manifest Oneness in all your corresponding thoughts, words, actions, and feelings.

---

3 A Course in Miracles (Foundation For Inner Peace, 1975, 1985, 1992), T-2.VII.6:1&2

4 A Course in Miracles (Foundation For Inner Peace, 1975, 1985, 1992), T-6.II.10:7

The way of Truth and Oneness is found through God's perfect laws. His Will is His law, which is Truth, Oneness, innocence, love, peace, and joy for all. Through God's unconditional love you are free to create yourself and your life as you choose. Surely, the more loving you are, the more you will *be love* and *be joy*.

Being in the world you will experience God's Oneness and love through the law of cause and effect. When I said, "It is done unto you as you believe,"[5] I stated this law. It is true that the happenings in your life are caused by your thoughts and beliefs. So, what you accept in your mind is the cause of your experiences and the resulting effects.

In so being, your manifestations are the corresponding effects that always mirror the cause. Being your Self you may express God's unconditional love as cause. Love creates your life in tandem with your Father and allows you to *be an extension of God*.[6] The closer you are to Him the more you experience your Self *being Truth* and *being One*.

Through this teaching you will understand that there is only One real cause or source and that is God or love. And there is only one real effect, and that is the Christ.

Upon contemplation of your life and state of affairs, you may see that change is called for. In this case you may shift your beliefs or cause and choose again. This freedom is the Father's gift unto you and your saving grace.

Surely, almost everyone desires to have a relationship with God, because He has placed a part of Him Self within every heart and mind. As you intentionally think and choose to *be* each New Beatitude you will experience God or love being the cause of your thoughts, words, and

---

[5] Matthew 8:13
[6] A Course in Miracles (Foundation for Inner Peace, 1975, 1985, 1992), T-7.IX.3:1

actions. Then you will be who you are meant to *be,* and the effects will be miraculous!

To *be* is to believe in your divinity, express it, and do it. Belief, acknowledgment, desire, and thought are steps in *being*. As you acknowledge your Truth by being these New Beatitudes intentionally, you will *be* who you really are. *Being remembrance, being awakened,* and *being aware* of your higher Self as well, all you need do is *be!* Being Spirit expressing as your Self, you may also practice each New Beatitude by being it, expressing it, expanding it, feeling it, and giving it away to another.

In this moment of Self-realization you will be close to God and me. This is God's plan for you, so you may be God's character and an extension of His Self. Your greatest potential awaits as you are in a close relationship with your Father and me. In this way you fulfill your soul's longing, vision, plan, and belief in Self-actualization, Oneness, and being.

You will find these New Beatitudes to be the essential teachings of the Spirituality that I embody. Spirituality is not religion, since religion is what man has done with my teachings. Spirituality also does not recognize sin, fear, and death; rather, it emphasizes innocence, love, and eternal life.

Essentially, Spirituality is a longing for God and communication with Him. It is being in a relationship with God, and making that relationship a priority in your life.

Spirituality is being of the Spirit, or being inspirit, which is the light of your divine Self. It is the intuition that life is more than it appears to be on the surface, and the courage to look within your Self for the answers that you seek. It is the commitment to discern your real life, identity, and purpose by experiencing, expressing, expanding, evolving, and *being* it now. Albeit, it has been said that your soul or Self doesn't evolve, but it does advance in awareness as life evolves.

Howbeit, you are Spirit within a physical body having a human experience, playing the game of life in order to understand your true identity, which is love, and your purpose, which is to *be love*.

You have chosen the Earth plane in which to expand love, practice forgiveness, explore contrast, and express your divinity so as to evolve and reside in a higher realm of Heaven.

Being the Christ temple is being the embodiment and consciousness of unconditional love. It is being human and divine with no separation, and this is what The New Beatitudes inspire you to *be*.

So you will be human and divine in One body, *being the Christ* temple, who is immune to external forces and enabled by the only power that is, being All that is. Yielding to the infinite and invisible power of All gives you dominion through grace. *Being grace* you live not as you but as Christ, *being the Christ* temple that embodies Spirit with your name, *being I Am*.

The harmonic convergence of your Self and All that is, *being One* within the One, as One, is the intention of your birth and the spiritual manifesto of a life well lived.

Quite simply, you have forgotten who you are so you may play and dance within the variety of extremes and opposites. Throughout your explorations, expansions, and expressions you will hopefully remember who you really are. The challenge is to close the gap between the physical and divine selves to *be One* Self. And thus you will be divinely human!

In other words, being in a physical body you are in the arena of duality, or external influences and forces beyond yourself. Yet the physical body is not who you are; the body is just your vehicle, I Am your guide, and The New Beatitudes are your map on this journey of spiritual discovery, definition, and Self-actualization.

Hopefully, early in the process you will *be awakened* to the Truth of the glorious adventure of life, so you may rise up and fulfill God's plan. *Being an extension of God* and *being One*, you have all the power you need to reconcile your seeming separation from your Father. Surely, you are One and never alone, and completely whole and capable, having everything and being everything. You are all light with no darkness, there is nothing to fear because there is no death, and the Truth will set you free to *be* who you are created to *be*. Verily, *being One* you influence and affect everyone by your light and vibration, so *be the light* and be inspiration. Surely, you may cancel out your false beliefs, realize your divine Self and *be allowing* of it now.

Spiritually expressing your divine Self, your will *be responsible* for your feelings and the truth they reveal. Many times you must feel the unwanted to release it and *be free* to feel better. You will also be introspective and *be aware* of the clarity of your divinity and attributes thereof. As you attune to how you feel, and why you feel a certain way, you can understand what is important to you and *be aligned* energetically with that good feeling as often as possible.

Acknowledging the thoughts and feelings that give you the greatest love, you might focus and fine tune them more often to love, essentially *being allowing* and *being aligned* with more love. *Being love* will align you with The 114 New Beatitudes which are aspects of love, and thus you will whole heartedly experience your Spirituality and divine Self.

On the other hand, if you discover pain and anger beneath your feelings, you might excavate the hurts and responsible variables thereof, and practice healing them by *being forgiveness.*

Being a creator and *being responsible* for how you feel are important steps in being Spiritual, connected, and joyous. Another step is to *be aware* of your fear as illusion, since it's a product of the ego and not real. Therefore, you can release it as misperception by asking to *be directed by the Holy Spirit* in forgiving it and creating new thought patterns. You may also ask the Holy Spirit to be in the holy instant often, where you leave time and space to *be remembrance* of all as Spirit and One.

Surely, your beliefs and intentions are your responsibility. But, thankfully, you can change your perspective any time and see things differently, if you find that it is not serving you well.

The outcome is always sure as you surrender the situation and allow me to direct your path. So *be surrender* and *be detached* from your personal attachments to the outcome, *being abiding* and *being trust* that I will awaken you to the holy grandeur of every present moment. These keys to Spirituality will further unlock your ability to overcome illusion and *be now,* so *be* it.

Likewise, I will say a few words about the title of this book, *Spirituality for the Common Man.* By the word "common" I mean the whole community of mankind, being all of the usual and ordinary people who are extraordinary because they have chosen to express and experience now upon Mother Earth.

The common man and common woman are courageous in their decision to incarnate at this time, ushering in a new Spiritual awareness of thought and being. They are embracing a new mission and seeing with holy vision. Even more, they are desiring lives of purpose and meaning beyond themselves.

The New Beatitudes have been called forth by a collective desire to be magnitude and expansion beyond the world's limitations. They have manifested here now by the longing of many hearts to *be now*.

Herein, I have come unto you through my messenger, Keith. In my lifetime as Jesus Christ she was known as Sarah. She travelled with the women who cared for the twelve disciples and me, protecting us from the Roman soldiers.

Now, she desires to inspire mankind to *be* The New Beatitudes, so the Sons and Daughters of God will *be remembrance* of their Father as my Self and their Selves.

Indeed, these New Beatitudes are the way to know the Father through the Son. Beloved, so *be* it.

1. Be God's Will. Blessed are you *be God's Will*, by acknowledging the Father as your Father now. God's Will is your true will, so do not deny your real Self. Beloved, honor and acknowledge God's Will and it will be done and accomplished in you. God's glorious Will, Spirit, inheritance, and character is Truth, Oneness, innocence, love, peace, and joy for all His Sons and Daughters. God's Will is reflected in His unconditional love and many aspects of The New Beatitudes as well. Surely, God's Will is far more wonderful than anything you might imagine, since it ensures all things are possible and working for you supernaturally. In the natural world things might appear unlikely and limited. Yet God's dominion is powerful above all things, because He is All That Is. Verily, may you be the common cause for the common man by *being God's Will now*.

2. Be God's Glory. Blessed are you to *be God's glory* as His beloved Child. The Father is great, powerful, gentle, and magnificent, and so are you, *being an extension of Him* as His beloved Child. Your innocence and love is God's glory that corrects all illusions. God's love is your power to *be joy, be peace, be whole,* and *be healed.* Further, God's glory is the magnanimous character, virtue, wisdom, goodness, light, and beauty of His being that you reflect, *being the Christ* temple as your Self. Be thrilled to glorify and behold the Creator and Source of all life, by valuing His invitation to be close to Him, love Him, and honor Him. Being a true, positive extension of His magnificent character and being is the intention of your life, your destiny to fulfill, and transformative power and glory that you may *be now.*

3. Be I Am. Blessed are you to *be I Am* as the One Son and beloved Child of the Father. In the beginning there was God, *being I Am* that I Am.[7] I Am is who you are also, *being One.* I Am is your fully evolved soul as well, yet as you express its fullness and perfection I will say that your experience of Self is evolving. So, recognize I Am as the powerful energy that creates all things, and declare your divine Self by saying "I Am" before whatever you desire, because I Am is the way God creates in words. Clearly, the words you think or speak following "I Am" create what will be, so *be intentional creation, be healed, be joy,* and *be peace. Be aware* of your divinity, Think with your divine Mind, and speak deliberately and positively to command your greatest destiny now. Monitor your thoughts and cancel out anything negative that you do not wish to experience, since you create with your thoughts. You may *be I Am* that, I Am as you practice and declare the "I Am" Statements of Being included in the appendix, and so may you *be now.*

---

[7] Exodus 3:14

4. Be One. Blessed are you to *be One* of the One as I Am. You are divinely interconnected with all life as One. Your Father is and always will *be One*, even as His Children think themselves to be separate from Him in the world. Surely, there is only One soul that is all life, so honor all life as One. *Being One,* you will see God in all or not at all. *Being One,* you are also privy to the Divine Self intelligence live stream that Source continually provides, and you may tune in or not. You choose your perspective, what you believe, and who you will be. Oneness is who you are. Whether you surrender, allow, and align with it is your choice. Albeit, *being One* is the power and momentum of Source as your Self, and so may you *be*, beloved. If you choose to ignore God and thwart a relationship with Him you will not experience the top of the world joy, power, and thriving awareness that is yours as One. You otherwise will look for completion within the world, yet not find it, since it resides within your Self and not within the world of illusions. Furthermore, quantum physics proves you can envision someone healed in your mind and they will be, because all is One. On the other hand, being separate and not living up to your highest Oneness potential is a form of hell. When it's all said and done, everything is known in the afterlife. Then and there you might wish to delete and reprogram your choices, because in your life review you feel how you made others feel, for better or for worse. Surely, what you do unto another you do unto God and your Self, because they are your Self and they are you. So have a we mentality rather than a me mentality. Finally, being connected to God I saw only Oneness and wholeness within all. So I was able to heal others, and so may you *be*.

5. Be Truth. Blessed are you to *be Truth* as I Am that I Am. Truth is your Father's Will and Thought and it states that only what God creates is real.[8] Thus God's reality is Spirit or Self, Oneness, love, Truth, joy, wisdom, and Heaven. The understanding of God's Mind as your mind, and God's life as your life is Truth. Verily, your individual power is proportionate to your consciousness of Truth, so *be Truth* and *be empowered*. In fact, Truth gives you dominion over the physical world, which actually is illusion, difficulties, and sickness. Only that which is unseen is eternal and true reality. Truth is also comprised of the many aspects of unconditional love that are named in The New Beatitudes and exemplified as the Christ Self. On the other hand, the ego's perceptions are illusion and not real, being physicality, negativity, separation, sin, fear, judgment, attack, and death.[9] In Truth, Spirit only unifies, heals, and releases, so *be Truth, be One, be healed*, and *be free*. In effect, God's Oneness is Truth, so separation in any way, between any two is impossible; *being Truth* allows love to embrace all as One, and so may you *be*. Surely, only God exists and all else is illusion, so realize God as your Self by experiencing Truth, witnessing Truth, and *being Truth now*.

6. Be God's Child. Blessed are you to *be God's Child* and the beloved extension of the Father. God only creates like Him Self, just as your children resemble you. Thus, your character is that of the Father, being infinite glory, holiness, innocence, and goodness. Not even your belief that you are something else will change your divine heritage. I will further say that it is blasphemy to think of your Self as anything less than perfect, since you are of God and from God, within Him and an extension of Him. Albeit, haven't

---

[8] A Course in Miracles (Foundation For Inner Peace, 1975, 1985, 1992), PR, p. x
[9] A Course in Miracles (Foundation For Inner Peace, 1975, 1985, 1992), PR, p. x

I prayed the Lord's Prayer saying, "Our Father who art in Heaven" because God is the Father of All? Therefore, all of God's Children have equal, merited, and unlimited access to Him, being of Him; so depend on Him and *be One* with Him. Be as little children as well and be reliant upon God, knowing and realizing the power of the Son and his relationship with the Father. I call the Father Abba, because He is more than just a Father. He is the Source of all that is, and the life that is all as One. So behold your Oneness, honor your being, strengthen your belief, align your behavior, become your divine Self, and *be God's Child now* as the Father created you to *be*.

7. Be Eternal. Blessed are you to *be eternal* Spirit as I Am. Your Spirit or life force is alive, divine, formless, immortal, and unchanging, so it does not die. Your soul or God Self has lived many lifetimes and has chosen to be here now to experience and create anew. Energy cannot be destroyed; it just changes form, so your Spirit and soul live on. My resurrection is proof of eternal life, because I rose again from the dead on the third day. Furthermore, *being eternal* is the gift of a lifetime, since the ego's beliefs in death, fear, and judgment cease; and with nothing to hold onto, the ego vanishes. Thus, you will *be free* from the ego's illusion and insanity, look within, be everlasting, and *be eternal* by living every now moment mindfully. Lastly, please read the addendum in the back of the book of Keith's father, Harvey C. Lane Jr.'s near death experience, which you will find comforting and reassuring as proof of eternal life.

8. Be Holy. Blessed are you to *be holy* as your divine Self. Your holiness is the innocence and unconditional love that you are. It is also your Father's Truth and power that creates all things, and He shares it with you. Holiness must be shared, for you cannot *be holy* without your brothers and sisters. So, *be holy, be innocent,* and be blameless since your Father does not judge you. As you can see, you either believe in a love based thought system or a fear based thought system, *being holy* or being of the world, and the intentional choice is yours. So be committed to the Truth and holiness that is within all, and set the captives free! Actually, there is only one holy relationship, and that is between the God Mind and the Holy Spirit. When you intentionally choose to *be directed by the Holy Spirit* and be the individual God Mind or Christ Mind that you are, by being these New Beatitudes your Self, all your relationships are holy. Letting go of your belief in separation also confirms your relationships to *be holy,* because you are *being forgiveness* and *being One* as I Am. Surely, *being holy* you can do all things because you are the power of God as your divine Self.

9. Be Remembrance. Blessed are you to *be remembrance* of your Self as Spirit within a physical body having a human experience. Likewise, may you *be remembrance* of your Truth, *being an extension of God* and *being His beloved Child.* Your Father always sees you as His innocent Son and I Am, and thus all else is irrelevant. The real, divine Self will always remind you of who you truly are, if you will *be still* and listen. *Being remembrance* of anything that already exists is recreating it, so it may be experienced again in the game of life. So, *be remembrance, be awakened,* recall and honor who you really are, *being God's Child*; what you are, *being love;* and why you are here, which is to *be love* and *be forgiveness.* This is your true identity and purpose that you may *be remembrance* of and *be now.*

10. Be Awakened. Blessed are you to *be awakened, be remembrance,* and *be One* as your divine Self. Seeing with my eyes in holy vision you will wake up and behold the Truth of the Father that is your Truth also. Returning to Him in awareness as divine Spirit, you will *be God's Will, be God's*

Glory, and *be God's Child*. May you *be awakened* to the Holy Spirit who is your inner guide as well, and be sure that you are never alone. May you be awakened to *be the Christ* temple too, as your spiritual practice gains momentum. May you also *be vigilant* to *be remembrance* that for every five minutes you focus on *being Truth*, a thousand minds are awakened. Lastly, may the common man *be awakened* to the common cause and *be God's Will now*. So *be* it.

11. Be an Extension of God. Blessed are you to *be an extension of God* as your Father, the Father of All, divine Spirit, Source, and your higher, divine Self. Being infinite Creation, love, and light, the Father must extend Him Self unto you because love is expansive. Perfect love is unlimited so you are what the Father is too. Being Spirit, your identity is far more than a physical body. The body is reflective of the thoughts you think about and what you do to yourself, because you do everything to yourself. For example, if your thoughts are unhealthy then your body will be unhealthy. Actually, bodies are temporary housing and transportation tools for your Spirit, which is the real, eternal you. Most importantly, you are the One Mind and universal Intelligence of the Father, *being whole, being holy*, and being perfect. Even more, you may change your mind and attitude to *be Truth, be I Am,* and *be God's Glory* today. Then you will truly be God's resemblance, being, and character, by *being* The New Beatitudes or "*be* attitudes" now.

12. Be Now. Blessed are you to *be now* in this present moment. Now is what is and who you are as I Am. Everything that is real exists right now, so *be now* and not in the past or future. Even if you are reminiscing about the past or thinking of the future you are doing it right now. So, the past and future exist merely in thought, and right now is your only reality and point of power. Hence, *be now,* be brand new, *be responsible,* and do not allow your past beliefs or fears of the future to influence what is happening in the present moment. Even more, *be free* from worn out ideas that don't behold the magnificence of your Spirit presence, and interpret the happenings in your life in the way you intentionally choose right now. Beloved, don't wait for tomorrow, because now is your time to *be.*

13. Be Respectful of All Life. Blessed are you *be respectful of all life* by honoring the One soul in all living beings that is God and your divine Self. So do not kill unnecessarily or mistreat another without recognizing the consequences of your actions. *Being One,* you are the two-legged, four-legged, furred, finned, crawling, and winged animal and plant beings. These creatures fulfill their mission by teaching mankind to *be love* and *be forgiveness* unconditionally.[10] Furthermore, life is sacred, relationships are holy, marriage is to be honored, mothers and motherhood are to *be respected,* fatherhood is reverent, and elders are to be valued, as well as your being, divine Self, human self, inner temple, body temple, and word. You must also honor Mother Earth as a sacred, living being by appreciating, conserving, and preserving natural resources. Share, compost, recycle, reuse, reduce your consumption and waste, and stop using plastic bottles and bags. Help save the rain forest by supporting preservation groups now, plant as many trees as possible, and leave no carbon imprint.[11]

---

10 Sharon Pieroni Day, The Book, The Creator's Template for Eternal Life, (Create Space, Charleston, SC, 2010) p. 93
11 Channeled by Linda Schiller-Hanna

Chapter 2

Jesus Is God Personified

I am Jesus Christ and I am God personified as the physical representation of the Father. I am Emmanuel or God with you, within you, and as your Presence within me. I am also the Truth, innocence, and love of God as the One Son. I personify the wisdom of *being God's Will* as my will, by *being I Am*.

Beloved One, it is true that I experienced life as Jesus to become the Christ. The Christ Spirit is the divine presence within mankind, being the potential for perfection that is I Am. In so being, I desired to teach humanity the way of love and forgiveness, so you can *be the Christ* with your name. For I am not exclusively the Christ, since God's Mind is within All as All, and available to all as each individual intentionally chooses to believe, become, actualize, and be their divine, Christ Self.

Therefore, my legacy is of a man named Jesus, who knew him Self to be God personified, and thus he became the Christ. You can do the same, and be the same, by being Self-realized now as I Am.

Christ is the personification of God within every common man and woman. This divine, inward Presence infuses your being and seeks manifestation through your thoughts, words, actions, and feelings. Christ is also your whole mind minus the illusions. Christ is the pattern for Source perfection that you may *be now* as well, *being I Am*. In so being, may you *be willing* to open the door of your mind to *be the Christ* temple now your Self.

As you know, I have overcome the world by my complete faith in God. Accordingly, I have always been and always will be totally dependent upon my Father, because He is my power and strength. Thus, I have chosen to exchange my human strength for God's divine power and strength, by *being God's Will* as my will.

Being very close to me, you may call me Yeshua. This is my given Hebrew name and it means Messiah and salvation. Call my name often and I will always answer, because we share an intimacy no human contact may know. It is a supernatural connection and friendship between God and man, One and One, equal and equal.

Be remembrance that I have known you personally in every lifetime and for all time. I am aware of all of your thoughts, words, actions, and feelings, and all of your history and future. Beloved, it is important to realize that nothing is ever hidden, so do not hide from your Self, since everything is Self-evident.

May you also *be remembrance* that no one loves you quite as passionately as I do, because I love you as my Self. So, behold the rapture of our friendship, this Spirit connection between you and me.

There is no breath that I breathe without thinking of you, and no thought that is separate from you. So, *be joy* in our closeness because there is no distance between us in any way, nor will there ever be.

Being your holy Christ Self, you will *be intentional choice* to *be the miracle* in every thought, word, action, and feeling. So behold God's Son who is your savior behind every grievance, requesting you to *be love* and *be forgiveness* in every opportunity to *be*. For, those who are judged must be appreciated for the gifts they give you; offerings of Oneness rather than separation, acceptance rather than judgment, love rather than grievances, forgiveness rather than blame, and miracles rather than darkness.

And thus you will *be willing* to allow your adversary to be your Self in remembrance of Oneness, Truth, and Love. Since they are the catalyst that reverses the ego's thinking, littleness, and negativity that you are not. They are also the light that you are, shining in awareness of your power to save others as you save yourself.

As you can see, these New Beatitudes are the way that I Am God personified, being who you may *be now, being the Christ* temple as your holy Self. Beloved, so *be* it.

14. Be Resurrection. Blessed are you to *be resurrection* and overcome sin, fear, and death. My resurrection demonstrated eternal life and the divine Spirit that we all are. Resurrection is also very important because it signifies overcoming false beliefs to *be the Christ* and your divine purpose now. Further, *be allowing* of the Christ to *be resurrection* and be born within your now. Apparent death is resurrection as you rise up and release all that does not serve or become you. So, experience a metamorphosis and transformation through release, rebirth, and resilience, becoming and being your higher power now. Your Truth and innocence testify to your resurrection and that of your brother, who is God and your Self. So *be faith, be resurrection,* and dare to *be* The New Beatitudes your Self. Defy illusion and be raised from a shallow tomb of worldly belief to become and *be love now.* Beloved, rise from the ashes of the past, *be aligned* and *be Truth,* be born again, *be the light, be the miracle,* and *be resurrection* by the healing of your mind now.

15. Be the Christ. Blessed are you to *be the Christ* or the perfect, divine presence and fulfillment of God. *Being unconditional love* and *being unconditional forgiveness* you may *be the Christ* with your name, as you choose to *be.* The Christ is I Am that I Am, your soul, or your higher Self. *Being the Christ* is your true innate identity, consciousness, presence and fulfillment of God, *being the Kingdom of God,* as Joel S. Goldsmith so profoundly stated in his book, *The Infinite Way.* In every situation the Christ will always *be love, be forgiveness,* and *be One. Being the Christ* temple or embodiment is personifying the human self and divine Self in One body with no separation or gap, and this is my example and hope for all. *Being the Christ* you will always choose between littleness, weakness, and fear or the magnitude, strength, and unconditional love of Christ that you really are. Judging another calls upon your own littleness and weakness; but forgiving another calls upon the Christ in you, so *be the Christ* your Self. Even more, be a temple of love and do for others before yourself, give more than asked, go the extra mile, *be respect for all life,* and care for the less fortunate equally as yourself. Surely, your task is to realize your true identity *being the Christ* Child, the Christ temple, the Christ Self, the

Christ Mind, and the Christ consciousness, because there is only One and there is only love, and so may you *be*.

16. Be Authentic. Blessed are you to *be authentic* and be your true Self as an extension of the Father. Your divine, authentic Self is who you really are as I Am. Your innate, authentic power is far more profound than the external power of the world, because it is inherent within your Self as Source energy. Authentic power is *being the Christ* temple, or being human and divine with no separation, and this is what The New Beatitudes inspire you to *be*. Thus, it is yourself *being aligned* with your Self, or your personality *being aligned* with your soul, as Gary Zukov perfectly states in *The Seat of the Soul*. In so being, the harmonic convergence of yourself and All that is, *being One* within the One, is the intention of your birth and the spiritual manifesto of a life well lived. Herein, within One body and One Mind resides your only true power that is permanent, intentional, authoritative, and holy. Further, *be remembrance* that the things of the world may give you temporary, external power, but they don't define you, nor are they real or lasting. Even more, God has spoken over you as His beloved; thus His power and glory are within your DNA. So rise to your authentic, infinite, inspirational, spontaneous, powerful potential and *be now*. Lastly, any blocks to your greatest self-acceptance and authenticity may be removed by *being love* and *being forgiveness* now. So *be* it.

17. Be the Golden Rule. Blessed are you to *be the Golden Rule* by doing unto others as you would have them do unto you. I ask you to *be the Golden Rule*, because all is One and there is no separation in the One, so *be One*. Indeed, what you do to another you do to God and your divine Self. And what you do for another you do for God and your

Self. So do for all as One, and be for everyone, even those who smite you, because I love everyone and *being an extension of God,* so should you. May you also love those whom the Father loves, being everyone. In so being, you will love your enemies because love is the only thing that heals, and love is who you are, so *be love.* Since judgment creates enemies, I ask you to *be non-judgment, be love, be forgiveness,* and have no enemies. Instead lavish your adversaries with gentleness and kindness, demonstrating the way to *be.* Surely, love is what everyone desires, and you are the One to *be love now!* Even more, may you do for others before you do for yourself, and then I will do the same, and give the same unto you. So *be* it.

18. Be Salvation. Blessed are you to *be salvation* and already saved, because you are God's beloved Child. You may believe that you are sinful and that you must be saved and delivered from hell. But, hell is here on Earth without *being love* and *being forgiveness.* Thus, you save yourself by your own love and forgiveness in every now moment. Albeit, salvation is being your true identity which is Spirit and not a body. So, *be acceptance* and *be salvation* in the realization that God created you as you are, *being innocent, being love,* and *being holy* as is. The fact that God created you as an extension of Him Self, and that you will always find your way back to Him is your salvation. So, you are not what you have created yourself; instead, you remain as God originally created you as your Self. Gratefully, this is your Truth and salvation, beloved. Finally, *be salvation* by realizing you do everything to your Self, *being One* for all as One.

19. Be Renunciation. Blessed are you to *be renunciation* of the ways of the ego and the world to *be the way* of love. The ego furthers judgment, fear, separation, negativity, and death, so it is not real. Yet, knowledge of the Truth sets you free to *be*. So, believe in God and Truth rather than the ego and illusion and *be Truth now*. Being the common cause for the common man by *being God's Will* is *being renunciation* of judgment and unforgiveness, and so shall you *be*. *Being renunciation* is being dominion over the world as well, by *being the strength* of Christ that overcomes all negativity. Lastly, *be renunciation* by changing your perspective and changing your mind, so your reality changes now.

20. Be the Way. Blessed are you to *be the way* and *be aligned* with the One Mind of God. The way is Truth, innocence, love, and forgiveness for everyone and everything, every time. Being Spirit in a physical body you are a holy extension of the Father, and not the littleness that the world has impressed upon you. So *be in the world but not of the world*, and fulfill your divine mission by *being love* as I Am. I have embodied love and forgiveness in my lifetime as Jesus Christ, *being the way* for all to see and *be*. It is clear that this world needs you to *be the light, be the miracle*, and be inspiration to all who are your Self beneath an illusionary exterior. Surely, the way is a living teaching of God personified, *being the Christ* in service to mankind; so *be the miracle worker, be a teacher* of love and forgiveness, and *be now*.

21. Be the Light. Blessed are you to *be the light*, love, and joy of the Father. When your will is God's Will[12] you will *be the light*. *Being the light* is the way to be Spirit and not a body, so be connected, *be eternal, be innocent,* and *be an extension of God*, which is who you really are. You will also *be the light* by *being non-judgment* and letting go of grievances. Light is the radiant energy and purpose of Spirit, being the innocence and love that you are. So *be One,* be connected to God

---

12 A Course in Miracles (Foundation For Inner Peace, 1975, 1985, 1992), T-11.III.3.3

and me, be in close relationships with us, be plugged in, fill your cup to overflowing and your light body to full, and allow your light to be bright, shining unto all who are your Self. You have agreed to be here now at this time, so you may *be the light* unto the darkness. Actually, your light filled thoughts heal your body, as you choose to focus upon God and *be healed*. Albeit, *be strength, be Truth, be courage,* shine your bright light unto the darkness, *be healed,* be an up lifter, be positive, be supportive, be complimentary, and constantly *be the light* in every intentional thought, word, action, and feeling now. Surely, you don't have to be right, just *be the light*.

22. Be the Atonement. Blessed are you to *be the at one-ment* by always choosing to *be love* rather than fear. Atonement undoes fear at its core by overcoming the ego by being unconditional forgiveness. So, acknowledge your original state of being by *being aware, being atoned,* and *being restored* to Oneness and innocence. See beneath the illusion to the holy One that is your Self and *be One* as I Am. *Be resurrection* and rise up to new heights of revelation, redemption, awareness, and beingness. *Be awakened* and *be remembrance* that all is One and all is your Self, and so may you *be*, beloved! Even more, *be authentic* and *be holy* in the atonement of all creation as all that is! The way of the atonement is unconditional love and forgiveness for everyone and everything, every time; thus it is a miracle for the miracle minded. Albeit, *being the atonement* you will *be intentional Thought* to *be One* and join all minds for the healing of all. Beloved, may you *be One* with all life by *being atoned,* rather than to be separate and think with the ego which is nothing, nobody, no one and no way.

Chapter 3

My Intentions Are Love and Forgiveness

As Jesus Christ, my intentions are love and forgiveness, and my example is one of love and forgiveness. Verily, love is the greatest power that is, being the creative energy of all that is. *Being unconditional love,* there is no judgment so there is nothing to forgive, so *be love.*

You are the power to *be* by the love that you are. In fact, in the beginning there was the Word, and the Word was God. God is love, so the Word that created all things was love. *Being an extension of God,* you are love too. *Being love* as your Self, it is essential to remove the blocks that obstruct your love from flowing fully. Realizing fear to be unreal and surrendering it to the Holy Spirit, you may forgive all to be all that is, being unconditional love as I Am.

Your identity is love and forgiveness, your purpose is to *be love* and *be forgiveness,* and the answer to life is love and forgiveness. So it follows that love and forgiveness are the answers to all of your problems and the way for mankind to change for the better. Even more, problems arise when you do not believe only in love. If you will only *be love*, you will have no problems. `

My intentions are for you to shift your perspective so you will be certain that *being love* and *being forgiveness* are the ways to *be.*

From here on within these pages, I will say *be love* many times. Yet my meaning is for you to *be unconditional love,* or true, perfect love. And when I say *be forgiveness* I am asking you to *be unconditional forgiveness,* or true, perfect forgiveness. This is being holy vision and standing on holy ground.

The Father's love is unconditional, and so may yours be. True, unconditional love holds no grievances against another.[13] Grievances are derived from judgment and guilt, and they verify a belief in separation and the ego.

Grievances are also a product of your human mind, and not God's Mind or the One Mind that you truly are. So think about this beloved, as you profess to love another, yet judge and find fault in them.

Grievances are formed by your illusions, which are outdated, judgmental thoughts in your egotistical mind. Grievances are also products of fear so they are not real. Holding grievances is a denial of the love that you are, since it promotes separation and pain.

---

[13] A Course in Miracles (Foundation For Inner Peace, 1975, 1985, 1992), W-pI.68.1:1

Holding grievances is also hurtful to you and those you judge. The only way to let grievances go is to *be nonjudgment* and *be forgiveness*. By allowing grievances to surface in your awareness, you may identify and forgive them all and thus *be unconditional love*.

Being love is also being fearless, since fear is illusion and not real. Only God's Creations are real, so your eternal Spirit can neither hurt nor be hurt[14] by anything. Learning to be unmoved by the judgments and attacks of the world is an important lesson and one that *being true forgiveness* will teach you.

Furthermore, *being love* you will help your brothers and sisters in every possible way. So, give to receive, since giving and receiving are the same.[15] If you are unhappy, you should question what you are withholding and not giving. Then give, *be service,* and uplift all. You may also *be intentional choice* to care for the less fortunate as your Self, serving the sick, starving, forgotten, mistreated people, animals, and living creations of the planet, by *being love* and *being service now.*

Herein, may you *be love* in every situation and if there is ever a question of loving or not, you will *be love* anyway. Love also places the beloved and their needs first, and only in this way is love fulfilled. Choosing love first and asking God for help, you will receive guidance and shift your perspective to the way of love. Even more, when the beloved isn't at their best, love steps in to comfort and protect, putting the beloved's needs before its own. Love yields and doesn't have to have its own way as well, especially because

---

14 A Course in Miracles (Foundation For Inner Peace, 1975, 1985, 1992), T-6.I.19:2

15 A Course in Miracles (Foundation For Inner Peace, 1975, 1985, 1992), W-pII.225.1:1

it is the way. *Being unconditional love* for another, regardless of their actions or opinions is *being remembrance* of the Oneness and sacredness of love that I Am.

Likewise, it is noteworthy to realize that the beloved must drop the shield of defense to let love in and *be loved*. Being vulnerable, *being open-minded*, and *being surrender* to the inherent, infinite love that is within all and around all is necessary, so one may receive love. Christ always loves, so *being the Christ* with your name you will gently and patiently make the beloved feel safe, worthy, and whole. Tenderly and compassionately love moves through thoughts, words, actions and feelings to embrace the beloved as its own, It Self, and One.

Finally, *being unconditional love* asks you to extend yourself beyond your comfort zone. Love naturally removes blocks and dissolves boundaries with the gentleness and tenderness of I Am. So *be I Am* and *be intentional choice* to love no matter what, because what matters most is how well you love.

Verily, I ask you to *be unconditional forgiveness* as well. True forgiveness recognizes that you are not separate from your Father or any living being. Thus, there is no sin and all sins are forgiven.[16] Beloved, you have made choices in your experiences but you have not sinned. So *be true forgiveness* and forgive automatically rather than judge automatically.[17]

On the other hand, the love of the ego is conditional. It is the love of the world that is temporary and qualified. It seeks completion by joining with another. Yet, you don't need anything outside of your Self because you lack nothing.[18]

---

16 A Course in Miracles (Foundation For Inner Peace, 1975, 1985, 1992), W-pII.1.1:3&4
17 A Course in Miracles (Foundation For Inner Peace, 1975, 1985, 1992), T-6.II.5:5
18 A Course in Miracles (Foundation For Inner Peace, 1975, 1985, 1992), T-1.V.4:4

Likewise, the forgiveness of the ego is similarly incomplete. It sees guilt and overlooks it, by judging supposed sin and making it real.[19] It also believes in fear, conditions, and attachments, so this is not true forgiveness.

You can overcome the ego by seeing it for what it really is: nothing. So cease to believe in it and forgive it all. *Be remembrance* and *be joy* in being sane, by thinking with your One, right Mind or the part of your Mind where the Holy Spirit lives. And remember that everyone makes mistakes, so *be compassion* and *be mercy* for all who are your Self, *being One*.

Even more, *being love*, you may easily release past complaints and judgments also, by forgiving all. But very often this is not the case, so you might monitor your thoughts and feelings and *be practice being forgiveness*.

Being Spiritual, introspective, and forgiving you will *be aware* of your feelings and the clarity they reveal. Understanding how you feel and why you feel a certain way, you can acknowledge the thoughts that bring you the greatest joy and tune yourself to *be joy*, like you tune a radio or TV channel. So focus on what makes you blissful for as long as possible, feeling joyful and *being joy*.

If you feel pain beneath your feelings, you may examine the hurt and why you feel that way. Anger will develop if you ignore the hurt and powerlessness you have experienced. Anger is not justified since you are love and One with all, so *be love, be non-judgment,* and *be One*. Furthermore, as you look directly at the problem and *be practice being forgiveness* of yourself and all concerned, your pain, anger, and possible resulting addictions will cease and *be healed*.

It is good to also ask God to heal your mind and *be directed by the Holy Spirit* in *being unconditional forgiveness*

---

19 A Course in Miracles (Foundation For Inner Peace, 1975, 1985, 1992), T-9.IV.4:4&5

and being the holy instant, which is letting go of the self and ego. Realizing all to *be innocent,* you will forgive everyone for everything every time, including yourself.

Being a creator, *being love, being forgiveness, being intentional creation,* and *being responsible* for how you feel are important steps in *being healed.* Surely, your beliefs and intentions are your responsibility. But, thankfully, you can change your perspective any time and see things clearly in holy vision.

As you can see, you must intentionally choose your beliefs carefully. You may believe in God and love, or the ego and fear. Your choice will always be either love or fear, and the way will always be clear.

Thus, I give you these New Beatitudes which reflect my intentions of unconditional love and forgiveness for all as One. Beloved, so *be* it.

23. Be Love. Blessed are you to *be unconditional love* by holding no grievances or judgments against another or yourself. God's love is perfect, eternal, and real, and so must yours *be.* The heart is the space of awareness, alignment, and peace, so *be* from your heart as I Am. Where fear exists, love is missing, so *be love* and heal all. *Being love* you will *be free* of illusions, judgments, and blame; hence you will be positive, live from a higher vibration, *be the light* and inspire others, achieve your goals, make the world a better place, fulfill your soul's purpose and divine destiny, *be the Christ* with your name, and merge yourself and your Self to *be now.*

24. Be Loved by God. Blessed are you to be treasured and *be loved by God* as the beloved. There is nothing you can ever do to stop your Father from loving you, because He loves you as Him Self. All of the Father's creations are extensions of Him and One with Him, so make your relationship with Him the most important one in your life, since it is the foundation of your life. Accept God's love and acknowledge His mercy and kindness that is forevermore. Build your house upon the rock and embrace your Sonship that is the immeasurable gift of love's extension and inclusion as I Am.

25. *Be Love for God.* Blessed are you to *be love for God* as your Father. The greatest commandment is to *be love for God*, because you are an extension of Him as His beloved Child. Loving, knowing, and praising God passionately enables you to *be joy*; thus the world will disappear into the illusion that it is and Heaven will be real now. *Be aware* also that no matter what you have experienced, your Heavenly Father has never hurt you. All hurt and drama are projections within your mind and not real, because only love is real, so *be love for God now.*

26. *Be Loved by Me.* Blessed are you to *be loved by me* and acknowledge my unconditional, eternal, and passionate love for you. I Am Spirit or the life force that activates your body and you live within me as your divine Self. Thus, you are never alone and you are not on your own. Your cares are my cares and everything that matters to you matters to me. So, *be trust* and know that I believe in you and love you as my Self. Finally, may you acknowledge your Self to *be loved by me* through my empowering gift of The New Beatitudes now.

27. *Be Love for Yourself.* Blessed are you to *be love for yourself* so you will be able to love others. Otherwise, you'll see within them the same fault that you find in yourself. You may also ask the Holy Spirit to direct you in *being love for yourself* by *being unconditional forgiveness*, since this is always the way to *be*. Some other ways to *be love for yourself* include setting up boundaries, respecting yourself, learning to say "no," taking care of your body temple, choosing your friends carefully, asking for help if you need it, not giving up your power or control, relaxing more, being in the flow, thinking before you speak, and emphasizing your accomplishments. Verily, you may *be love for your divine Self* by accepting your holiness, innocence, and worthiness, because you are enough, you are here for a reason, you matter, and you are fulfilling your divine mission to *be*. All the more, *being practice* and *being intentional* in being The New Beatitudes is the way to *be love for your Self* as I Am. Finally, may you release your self-doubt and *be remembrance* that in every situation you did the best you could at the time, beloved.

28. Be Love for One Another. Blessed are you to be brotherly love for all as One, by *being love for One another*. I have said that the second greatest commandment is to love your neighbor as your Self. To dislike others is to dislike yourself, because you always find yourself in another. So see your Self within others by looking into God's eyes and beholding the light within. *Be love* for those who don't love you by *being non-judgment* and holding no grievances against them. Be true to your destiny and do not be concerned with the judgments of others. Continue to *be forgiveness* of their opinions and be true to your Self, *being love* for them no matter what. *Be remembrance* that you can't change the world, but you can change your perspective and yourself. *Be love* also by realizing that love has to be given away and you can't save yourself alone. Certainly, you'll heal others by accepting God for them, loving them where they are, being sensitive toward them, and giving all to God for His Will to be done and accomplished now.

29. Be the One Mind. Blessed are you to *be the One Mind* and universal Intelligence of the Father. God's Mind is written with a capital "M" and God's Thought with a capital "T," which is Thinking with the One Mind of God. This is possible when you change your perceptions about reality and listen to your true voice of reason and sanity by *being Truth*. The separated mind is the place of the ego, your life stories, and individual roles that form your identity. *Being the One Mind* is being right Minded or Christ Minded in your beliefs, awareness, consciousness, and Thoughts by *being aligned* with God. You may also *be the miracle* as you intentionally join your Mind with others for the healing and blessing of all, *being the One Mind*. So be in your right Mind by Thinking thoughts that reflect God's being, nature, and character, by *being the One Mind, being the Christ,* and being The New Beatitudes *now.*

30. Be the Miracle. Blessed are you to *be the miracle* of love and forgiveness now. May you behold all things with my eyes in holy vision, rather than with physical eyes that judge, blame, and see guilt. Verily, you will receive a miracle when you read this book, or even parts of it. As you are willing to let go of your control, attachment, and will to *be God's Will*, you will *be surrender* and *be the miracle.* Realizing how deeply you are loved and cared for, you will *be confident* that I am rearranging time and space to guide, provide, bless, and inspire you to expect, receive, and *be the miracle.* Appreciating the power of your intentional Thoughts, you will *be the miracle* worker when you bless someone with your Mind. You will also *be the atonement* and *be the miracle* worker when you listen to me and perform the miracles I directly request. Most likely, this involves your *being love* and *being forgiveness* and inspiring others to be the same. Revelation soon follows with the aha moment that God is in you, for you, with you, by you, through you, you are within Him, and He is here now! Albeit, these dynamic keys to life will empower you to *be the miracle* as you realize Christ is your Self and the holiness that you are!

31. Be Joy. Blessed are you to *be joy* by *being God's Will now*. Joy is an aspect of the love that you are and the Truth of your divine Self, so it is permanent and real. This is the reason you may always *be joy* when things go awry in the world. Eternal joy does not come from material things, which are temporary and of the world. Thus, it is different from happiness, which is derived from the temporary and elusive. So don't worry, *be joy!* For, I have said that levity is good, so *be awakened*, lighten up, and *be joy*. Actually, *being love, being forgiveness,* and *being joy* increases your energetic vibration; so feel lighter, be buoyant, and *be free* by focusing on feeling good and *being gratitude now*. Joy is also your success and intentional choice, since the more love you give, the more joy you feel. You will especially *be joyous* being your higher power as the magnificent, perfect personification of the Father and the Christ. Howbeit, you may *be joy* by dissolving the ego and knowing me, depending on me, *being aligned* with me, *being sustained* and *being restored* by me, being within me, *being allowing* of your divine Self, and realizing your identity within God. And in so being, you will *be surrender, be appreciation, be the light, be the miracle, be salvation,* have a sense of humor, be positive, be fun, be adventurous, relax, giggle, go with the flow, release resistance, pay attention to the good and cancel out the rest, and make everything an opportunity to laugh, smile, dance, sing, and rejoice, since this is your true wealth, purpose, and time to *be now*. Finally, I say, find and *be* your Self, *be joy*, and end your despair.

Chapter 4

Why Forgiveness Is a Part of Me

Now I wish to speak of forgiveness, and why it is necessary in the world today. Certainly your Father hasn't condemned or blamed you for anything,[20] so you must not condemn and blame yourself.

God has not forgiven your sins because you are innocent and there is nothing to forgive. Sin is not real since it is a product of the ego and its false beliefs, and it is merely a call for more love. Innocence is the Father's energy and Presence, being the true state of mind of His Son,[21] so *be innocent.*

---

20 A Course in Miracles (Foundation For Inner Peace, 1975, 1985, 1992) W-p.I.46.1:1
21 A Course in Miracles (Foundation For Inner Peace, 1975, 1985, 1992), T-3, I.8:1

It is understandable that your supposed separation makes you fearful and afraid. So you project your unconscious judgment, guilt, blame, and hidden sin onto others. Yet you must forgive yourself, your perceptions, your illusions, and the past to *be unconditional forgiveness.*

In fact, to forgive means to overlook[22] and to love rather than to judge. So overlook what you think you perceive, and believe in the innocence of your brother and your Self that is the Christ Mind and true reality, *being forgiveness.*

Herein I desire to remind you that there is no world, and that the separation only happened in your divided mind. So, you must forgive others for what they did not do.[23]

This is true because you are still in Heaven where you project the world like a movie. This phenomenon is scientifically explained by Michael Talbot in his amazing book, *The Holographic Universe,* and I recommend it.

Usually you think forgiveness is necessary when someone does something unkind, unjust, or hurtful. But since the world is projected and not real, since it is illusion, nothing really happened so there is nothing to forgive. Illusions are projections and drama from separated minds, because only God's creations are real.

Actually, illusions are problems and anything fear based that expands without forgiveness. Illusions are derived from judgment and attack, and forgiveness is the only tool to dismantle the faulty projection and perception. *Being One* you will see all others as your Self, since

---

[22] A Course in Miracles (Foundation For Inner Peace, 1975, 1985, 1992), T-9, IV.1:2
[23] A Course in Miracles (Foundation For Inner Peace, 1975, 1985, 1992), T-17, III.1:5

there is no separation between any two beings. Everyone is you and all is One, so *be One* and *be forgiveness* and do not judge and attack another or you will feel the pain thereof.

Accordingly, you may *be remembrance* that time, cause and effect, and manifesting are beliefs of the world and not the Oneness of Heaven, which is your true Home. You may also recall that God is the only power, cause, effect, and choice for Truth, and that God's Children are innocent and sinless.

Therefore, the way to forgive others for what they did not do is to *be unconditional forgiveness*. Thus, you will not judge, blame, or attack another or yourself. You will also forgive automatically rather than judge automatically. Judgment makes you unhappy, since it is really a mirror of your own self-judgment, so *be non-judgment* and *be forgiveness*.

On the other hand, you may be good judgment by *being understanding* and discerning. Good judgment is developed through maturity, self-discipline, and wisdom, being a necessary trait in the world today.

Being non-judgment is an important key to forgiveness, since it is the way to transcend judgment. Since love doesn't judge, there isn't anything to forgive if you are *being love* and *being non-judgment*. But many people do judge, being caught up in negative habits that do not serve them. The miracle that heals judgment is gratitude, so *be non-judgment* and *be gratitude*. Instead of judging what might be or could have been, *be acceptance* for what is, *being God's Will* as your will, and being the common cause for the common man.

Similarly, self-judgment may block your abilities to *be love, be joy, be intuition,* and *be healed* because you think less of yourself than God does. These false conclusions are often times founded upon past ideas that are groundless and unrealistic. Being stuck in judgments you must forgive and replace them with God and accurate, positive choices to *be;* so *be aware, be forgiveness, be non-judgment, be intentional creation* and *be intentional choice* to choose again for the better.

The way to forgive and replace judgments is to *be still, be the light,* and connect with God by *being the One Mind, being allowing,* and *being aligned* with I Am. Envision God's light filling your body and your Self *being the light.* Declare the judgments that no longer serve you, *being renunciation* and *being surrender* of them now. Replace outdated beliefs with new ones that reflect your present moment awareness. *Be present, be grateful, be joy,* and *be acceptance* of your new desires and thank God for this now moment, *being joy,* being new, and *being now.* And continue to *be intentional Thought* by Thinking only what you desire to *be now.*

Likewise, there is great healing in *being acceptance* and *being gratitude,* which are life changing strategies and keys for success. As your attitudes shift to New *Be*-Attitudes of acceptance, non-judgment and gratitude, you'll experience higher levels and dimensions of surrender, allowing, peace, healing, detachment, and joy. No longer must you have your way, since your way is controlling and judgmental. Now you let go and let God, *being the way* of miracles. And so may you be well, *be well-being,* and *be,* beloved.

I must say once again that *being gratitude* is a very important key in *being forgiveness,* since it is the way to transcend judgment. Additionally, *being unconditional forgiveness* is the answer to all of your difficulties because it frees you from the world's illusion. It also releases fear and heals minds through true perspective and objectivity. As you release the past, your hurts, and feelings of powerlessness to *be forgiveness,* you will heal your judgment and guilt. Also,

Why Forgiveness Is a Part of Me

feeling and confronting pain and corresponding addictions causes pain to cease, so *be forgiveness* always.

You may also *be unconditional forgiveness* by allowing your mind to *be directed by the Holy Spirit*.[24] He is God's voice of Truth within you who heals your separated mind and corrects your thinking. This correction is only possible in your mind where the Holy Spirit replaces[25] your unconscious judgment and guilt with real Thoughts of innocence, love, and Oneness.

As you desire and ask the Holy Spirit for forgiveness and guidance, *being willing* to *be guided* and *be directed*, you will *be*. He delights in your call upon Him and always answers. Difficult relationships and circumstances will *be transformed* as you ask to *be directed by the Holy Spirit* in *being love* and *being forgiveness* rather than practicing fear, judgement, or attack. Ease and joy prevail when you continually ask the Holy Spirit to direct your decisions and always call upon Him for guidance, healing, and miracles.

In the moment you desire to *be willing, be surrender*, and request the Holy Spirit to intervene, he will shift the perspectives involved through creative, loving possibilities of release that change attack into love. *Being love* you'll see a way in holy vision to *be forgiveness* and release all from judgment and grievances. And asking the Holy Spirit to be close to you in a relationship, you will acknowledge your indwelling teacher and guide who always knows what to do, how to do it, and when to act. He is truly your closest friend and ever present source of comfort, support, and safety.

---

24 A Course in Miracles (Foundation For Inner Peace, 1975, 1985, 1992), T-9.IV.2:3 & W-p.ll.361-365.1:4

25 A Course in Miracles (Foundation For Inner Peace, 1975, 1985, 1992), W-p.I.23,4:4

After calling upon the Holy Spirit, you may *be still*, meditate, *be prayerful*, pay attention, and listen for God's words, dreams, whispers, suggestions, intuition, signs, signals, messages, visions, prophecies, wonders, or external coincidences that appear. For herein is your guidance and direction in the way to *be the miracle* of love and forgiveness.

While *being directed by the Holy Spirit* in any circumstance, you may ask "what would love do now?" And the Holy Spirit's answer will always *be forgiveness, be gentle, be compassion, be acceptance, be joy, be One,* and *be mercy,* along with the other remaining New Beatitudes. The peaceful Oneness of God's Will is the answer, derived from your internal request, prayer, written questions or spoken words. Even more, always *being forgiveness* of everyone and everything, including yourself is the Holy Spirit's continuous response to your call for more love and more forgiveness.

Essentially, the Holy Spirit will teach you to *be true, unconditional forgiveness,* and not the conditional forgiveness of the world. *Being the One Mind* as your Self, I work there alongside the Holy Spirit to heal your thinking as well. Making this a daily practice will allow you to *be peace* and *be healed,* so ask and receive the greatest guidance imaginable in *being love, being non-judgment, being the miracle,* and being inspired as I Am.

The steps in *being forgiveness* through the Unconditional Forgiveness Thought follow, which guide you in *being directed by the Holy Spirit. Be remembrance* that you are Thinking this with God and the Holy Spirit, so it is Thought with a capital "T." Whenever you experience any judgment, guilt, or negative thoughts you may identify them and ask the Holy Spirit for correction by following these steps:

Why Forgiveness Is a Part of Me

The Unconditional Forgiveness Thought

Think or say "I desire to…
1. *Be remembrance* that the situation is illusion and not real, because it is fear, judgment and guilt.
2. *Be responsible* and *be love* as cause of my creations.
3. *Be surrender* and let it all go.
4. *Be trust* in the Holy Spirit to heal my mind and correct my thinking now."

Then *be gratitude* for the Holy Spirit's healing and *be vigilant* in hearing His voice. Continually surrender painful, powerless, dramatic feelings that should be challenged and addressed. Unhealthy addictions and anger develop when pain goes unchecked, so *be aware* of your feelings and what they represent, and do not give your power away.

At the source of your addictions and cravings are the unaddressed wounds of powerlessness and unworthiness. As you acknowledge the source and cause of your pain, and forgive it all, you will *be healed*. In *being responsible, being non-judgment, being surrender, being forgiveness*, and *being aligned* with your innate wholeness, worthiness, and perfection you will *be healed, be free*, and *be now*.

The more you practice listening to the Holy Spirit the stronger your relationship with Him and the clearer His message. The more you welcome His presence and guidance, the more often you will experience the Holy Instant. This is where you stand on holy ground, by experiencing a shift from fear and judgement to love and miracles.

Finally, your body is a temple of the Holy Spirit, whom you have received from God. *Being an extension of God* you are not a body; you are the temple of the Holy Spirit and it is good to accordingly *be* so.

And in so being, these New Beatitudes are why forgiveness is a part of me. Beloved, so *be* it.

32. Be Innocent. Blessed are you to *be innocent* as God's holy Child. *Be remembrance* that God always beholds your original innocence, even as you are here upon the Earth creating, since sin is a product of the ego and therefore not real. Innocence is the Father's energy and Presence, being the true state of mind of His Son,[26] so *be innocent.* The Father's love is the energy and vibration of innocence, and this is what you are. Forget what you think anyone has done in the past, because God only sees the original innocence of His beloved Child. The ego and the world focus on your guilt and mistakes, but I focus on your innocence and good intentions. You must also respect the innocence of all living beings, honoring their divine mission to heal mankind by *being respectful of all life now.*

33. Be Forgiveness. Blessed are you to *be unconditional forgiveness* that does not judge or hold grievances against another. This is seeing beyond the veil of the world and the ego as I see. Indeed, what you thought your brother did never happened, because it was a perception in the world of illusion. Fear is powerless so *be free* and see things differently in holy vision, looking directly at your fear. Many times you fear redemption which is already yours, and you overlook the Oneness principle that the other One is really you. Further, *be open-minded* by denying guilt and judgment, since the happenings you imagine are mere projections of your thoughts. I say, don't fear the

---
26 A Course in Miracles (Foundation For Inner Peace, 1975, 1985, 1992), T-3, I.8:1

light, just *be the light* and be the marvelous Spirit that you are! Then ask to *be directed by the Holy Spirit* and allow Him to heal your mind and correct your thinking. Truly, those whom you forgive grace you with the most important gifts of all. Beloved, may you constantly *be the light, be the miracle*, and *be forgiveness* by being these keys to peace, healing, and fulfillment now.

34. Be Directed by the Holy Spirit. Blessed are you to ask, receive, listen, and *be directed by the Holy Spirit's* voice for God.[27] He is your internal guide and the voice of unconditional love, inspiration, and intuition who restores your mind, corrects your thinking, and directs you in the way to *be forgiveness*. So ask the Holy Spirit to help you forgive everyone, including yourself. And to give you the holy instant as well, where you reside in forgiveness as Spirit your Self. Herein, you let go of your personal identity to experience your Self as Spirit and rest in the peace and holiness of miracles, so be the holy instant often. All healing is of the Holy Spirit, so *be remembrance* of your Truth and identity in Christ and *be* it now, beloved. May you be sure to live securely in love as well, because the Holy Spirit is present in all situations, all throughout the day. Whenever you find yourself being negative and in need of an attitude adjustment, ask the Holy Spirit to heal your mind and direct you in *being love*. Make every decision with Him and ask what miracles you may perform this day. *Be remembrance* that a single request is sufficient, heard, appreciated, and granted. You will also be truly efficient when you appreciate and befriend the Holy Spirit as your inner guide, while creating in union with the universe. Moreover, may you *be allowing* of your life to be a testament

---

[27] A Course in Miracles (Foundation For Inner Peace, 1975, 1985, 1992), CL-6.1-4

to my love and the Holy Spirit's guidance. Finally, ask, *be willing, be trust, be allowing, be surrender*, and *be faith* in the Holy Spirit to align all with the unconditional love, forgiveness, and joy that I Am and you are now.

35. Be Non-Judgment. Blessed are you to *be non-judgment* as I Am, and refrain from finding fault in others. Judgment comes from the ego's superior sense of self, rather than from the One Mind that sees all equally. Judgment is projection, anger, and blame, being an illusion of the world and duality. It furthers separation by condemning and correcting others. Judgment blocks awareness of the love and light that you are, and of your brother's light as well. Judgments are grievances that make it impossible to realize and be your Self, so *be non-judgment*. Judgment breeds discontent as well, because when you attack another you attack your Self, so *be One, be love,* and *be non-judgment*.

36. Be Acceptance. Blessed are you to *be acceptance* of the Truth that there is a Higher Power who loves you and desires your love. May you also *be acceptance* of God as your Father, and your brothers and sisters as your Self. Further, may you accept all living beings as One Spirit and One soul, by *being respectful of all life*. More so, *be acceptance* and *be now* in every present moment, changing nothing by living life authentically and profoundly. It is good to note that there is power in acceptance, for as you accept and *be God's Will* rather than your own will, new opportunities for growth and expansion show up. From this point of power, you free the ego by *being detached* from your way and the outcome, to be the way in ease and understanding. Herein, soul gifts appear that propel you to the greatest heights of success imaginable, oftentimes enlisting divine providence and power that would not have appeared in any other way, so *be acceptance*. I must also say that *being* *acceptance* requires courage and boldness, an allowance of being in the flow, clarity to recognize blocks to abundance, and forgiveness to dismantle them. The journey of acceptance also, most likely, will involve calling upon the Holy Spirit for the Holy Instant and me for whatever way we may comfort, support, and strengthen you, beloved. May you *be remembrance* that in *being God's Will* and *being acceptance*, all is well and expressing for the highest good of all. And very importantly, may you *be acceptance* of God's plan of dominion for your life and fulfill it, by *being love, being the light*, and *being renunciation* of the world to bless and heal all living creations. Finally, *be acceptance* of everyone, loving them right where they are and loving them anyway, as love is.

37. Be Compassion. Blessed are you to *be compassion* and brotherly love toward yourself, and all who are your true Self, *being One*. May you also walk in another's sandals feeling what they feel. For, as you deeply feel passion, understanding, concern, and empathy for another, you will also know it for yourself, *being compassion* and *being One*. In so being, may you care for others, make a difference, and be the change for all who are less fortunate and in need. *Be service*, be concerned, and share your conviction and hope that saves lives and restores joy as well. Furthermore, compassion is Oneness in action, and doing for others as you would have them do unto you, so *be compassion* and *be the Golden Rule now.*

38. Be Tolerance. Blessed are you to *be tolerance* and see the Christ within everyone. Thus, you will *be non-judgment* even when others judge you, for if you react and judge them you judge yourself. Judgment and intolerance infer that you can be dominated, and you cannot. No one has power over you unless you allow it. Further, *being tolerant* and *being allowing* of yourself to feel your feelings, and understand your emotions, you may accept whatever they are. Albeit, you may feel them for as long as necessary and then *be forgiveness* of all concerned including yourself, and let it all go, *being love* and *being non-judgment*. Being vulnerable and *being courage* to feel, you allow the pain to *be healed* and your resulting negative behavior to *be forgiven, be transformed* and be released. Even more, *be remembrance* that you are eternal Spirit so you cannot be harmed by anything in the world, so *be tolerance* and *be safe*.

39. Be Defenseless. Blessed are you to *be defenseless* and have no illusions that you must defend.[28] So do not react to the world's judgment and attack, because you do not have to defend yourself, acknowledge illusion, or be right. No one can hurt your eternal, innocent Spirit that cannot be offended. Only the ego takes offense, so *be non-judgment* and *be forgiveness*. Believing yourself to be a body rather than Spirit, separate rather than One, and alone rather than all as One, you will defend yourself; and this need not be! Verily, you will think it necessary to defend your own ideas rather than to *be trust* in the ideas you created in union with the Holy Spirit, so *be defenseless*. Also, being the strength of Christ and *being the light* of the world you have no need of defense. Thus, may you forgive judgments, weed your garden of all that must go, let no one have power over you, and *be safe* by *being defenseless now*.

40. Be Healed. Blessed are you to *be healed* by *being love* and *being forgiveness* unconditionally. All healing is through the Holy Spirit, so *be remembrance* of your Truth and identity and *be* it now. Furthermore, the body is an effect of your mind's thoughts, so be the cause of your well-being

---

28 A Course in Miracles, (Foundation For Inner Peace, 1975, 1985, 1992), W-pI.153.9:3

by changing your mind and releasing any meaning you give pain. Through the body you demonstrate love and light. Shining Spirit's light unto all, your body will reflect the light and be healthy, so *be the light*. Even more, you are Spirit, *being whole, being eternal,* being perfect, and *being well-being*. If there is any sickness, your thoughts must *be healed* by *being aligned* with God's Will as your will, only thinking what you desire to *be*, and cancelling out all fearful ideas. Specifically, may you *be Truth, be vigilant,* and *be intentional Thought* only, always *being aligned* with God. And so, stating, declaring, and being the "I Am Statements of Being" you will *be healed* and be a healer. Surely, the vibrational energy and frequency of Truthful Thoughts are far greater than those of your small mind; so your aligned Mindful Thoughts cancel out ego thoughts and healing manifests. Verily, as you *be love* for others and desire healing for them before yourself, you will *be healed*. Albeit, *being One* is the way to *be* in all your creations, since you experience your creations one way or another. Furthermore, it is interesting that the "ha-ha" energy of laughter resonates at 528 HZ; this is the Healing Frequency documented by Dr. Len Horowitz, so laugh more and *be healed*. Lastly, *be directed by the Holy Spirit* in *being forgiveness* and you will *be healed, be peace,* and *be joy now*.

Part Two

YOU WILL SEE WITH MY EYES

Chapter 5

If You Love and Forgive

Christ is God's Son and creation, and everyone is God's Child, so every common man and woman is the Christ with their name. Christ sees all in holy vision, beholding everyone as Spirit in a physical body. *Being the Christ* temple, you will embody and behold the holiness of all life, all things, all relationships, and all beings. In fact, there is nothing that is not holy, because God and Christ dwell within all as all. I have come to say that since the Father lives within all as all, everyone is Spirit embodied as a temple. Your Christ temple is Self-evident as you create your Self *being love* and *being forgiveness* in every thought, word, action, and feeling.

As you see holiness in every common man and woman, and all common things, you witness with holy vision the truth of being and the sacredness of life. Holy vision is seeing with my eyes that behold all life as sacred, all as One, all are connected, everything matters, everything is interconnected, everyone is innocent, and all are standing upon holy ground *being One, being Truth*, and *being extensions of God*. And thus, you may truly see.

I have come to awaken mankind to life's sacred reality within all as One, and your divine destiny to be human and divine in one body as your Self. Because there is no separation from Source, all life is an extension of God in its physical form. Acknowledging this and being this is the intention of your birth and so may you *be!*

Albeit, you are here to expand love, practice forgiveness, explore differences, and express your divinity as the fully awakened Christ temple with your name. And thus you experience the unity of life, the vastness of the One, and the sacredness of every moment being fully alive.

Holy vision is the way to view all of your brothers and sisters with my eyes. It furthers truth by teaching you to be true perception. When you see my face and likeness within everyone, and lead with love, you heal my heart, restore my joy, and see in holy vision as your Self.

So see with holy vision and behold God within all living beings. Look into the eyes of another and see the innocence and love of the light within. Even more, see God within all the animals and *be respectful of all life*, doing for them as God and your Self. See Spirit reflected in the life force that is each particular soul's journey and longing for Itself.

Your false beliefs or projections make your perceptions. In your separate mind you think that the physical

If You Love and Forgive

world is real, but only God and His Creations are real. Thus you are dreaming a dream that you must awaken from, so *be awakened* and see with holy vision.

Actually, you created the planets and the world with your Father, *being One*. Being multidimensional and infinite creation, you decided to experience some excitement and drama in the physical realm of duality or opposites. So you chose to descend into matter, and thus you are Spirit expressing within matter.[29]

Being remembrance of your Spirit and Oneness is now your mission. Thus, you may *be love* and change your past egotistical patterns of behavior. Make a point to *be aware* of and monitor your thoughts and Think before you judge or attack another. Also, *be intentional choice* to hold no grievances and *be non-judgment* by cancelling out your perceptions immediately by *being love*.

Howbeit, to *be love* if you have judged, you might ask? And I answer saying, your judgment is within you and not the one you have judged. Your ego or small self has judged, and now you must realize you have chosen to judge. Realizing your decision, you may *be intentional choice* to *be forgiveness* of yourself and what you judged. Realize judgment is illusion, drama, guilt, and littleness, so choose again and do not allow it to separate you from God's love.

You might practice *being forgiveness* even more by asking to *be directed by the Holy Spirit*. He dissolves your judgment and guilt and blesses you with the holy instant.[30] This is the present moment that you renounce the ego and its illusion to finally *be peace*. For certainly you do everything unto

---

[29] Judith Coates, Jeshua The Personal Christ, Volume II, (Oakbridge University Press, 1996) p 33 & 35
[30] A Course in Miracles (Foundation For Inner Peace, 1975, 1985, 1992), T-16.VII.6:1

yourself, *being One*. You might also ponder this point as you consider the resistance that has appeared in your life, and the possibility that you called it unto yourself for a particular reason. Since the other is your Self and God, and you are responsible for everything in your life, you might *be forgiveness* automatically since there truly is no world.

Thus, I would like to emphasize the value of the holy instant, which is a great principle. In fact, it is profound because it allows you to collapse time and move forward into a new place without the ego, judgment, grievances, or drama. The beauty of the holy instant is asking the Holy Spirit for it, ascending above the illusion, and dropping back into time and space where the drama is left behind. Since you are Spirit and a creator in a physical body, you can perceive everything from a vertical perception, rather than from a horizontal, timely perception as you do now, being in the world.

In the space of the holy instant, you experience being Spirit with no physical baggage. You see the world as illusion and make believe, or a projection of your thoughts, like watching a movie or TV show. You see it but it's not real, so choose your thoughts carefully.

Therefore, the holy instant allows you see the world differently. Realizing that fear is in your mind, that fear and guilt are not real, and that fear does not have any power over you, you will *be free!* So *be vigilant* and monitor yourself closely. Release all fearful and negative thoughts, *being surrender* and giving them to the Holy Spirit for correction. Furthermore, you are most afraid of your Truth, redemption, and atonement. The ego and small self think God's Truth is too good to be true, so you fear your divine magnificence and ability to *be now*, and this need not *be!*

If You Love and Forgive

Thus, being in the holy instant you will *be love for God, be love for me, be directed by the Holy Spirit, be still, be openminded, be renunciation* of the world that does not exist, *be transformed* by Truth and love, and *be resurrection now*. Beloved Child, ask and *be allowing* of the Holy Spirit to give you the holy instant, so you may *be* the holy instant. Because now is the time to rise up, shine, *be the light, be love, be remembrance* of who you really are as Spirit, and create accordingly.

Now just ask and it is given! Ask me and your inner guide to direct your mind in *being forgiveness* so fully that you undo your negative thought system to think only loving and forgiving thoughts in the holy instant your Self. Here you may *be* and stay as often as you like; just ask, *be allowing, be aligned* and be in perfect connection and communication with Spirit. So *be* it!

The Holy Spirit will also transform your worldly relationships into holy relationships. Relationships teach you to *be One* with your brother and sister who are God and your Self, so *be forgiveness*. They also teach you your greatest lessons and give you your most important gifts. Thus, you will see your relationships thrive as you practice *being forgiveness* of all illusions.

As you continuously ask the Holy Spirit to heal your separated mind, you will be positive, *be joy*, and be completely dependent upon me. You may also *be practice* of the Unconditional Forgiveness Thought in every situation where you feel the least bit negative, so you will *be healed* and *be the Atonement*. More so, *be remembrance* that you always have a choice between Truth and illusion. You will truly *be free* as you choose to *be God's Will* as your will, and thus you will *be salvation now*.

Being love and *being forgiveness* you will be holy vision and be these New Beatitudes now. Beloved, so *be* it.

41. Be Vigilant. Blessed are you to *be vigilant* for God and His Kingdom.[31] Vigilance is intentional focus and remembrance of God by *being aligned* with Him. Specifically, *being still* for five minutes and concentrating on God, you will inspire thousands of minds to *be aligned* with God's Truth and being. Verily, *being vigilant* is your power to *be forgiveness* and *be salvation*, and for all minds to ask, receive, hear, and *be Truth now*. Even more, be purification and *be vigilant* in overcoming the ego, illusion, fear, and separation. May you especially *be vigilant* in *being discipline* in your Thoughts and choices to *be now*. So release others from the chains that bind them and heal the world by *being vigilant, being aligned, being still, being the light, being the miracle,* and being the change now!

42. Be Whole. Blessed are you to be Spirit and *be whole*, which is undivided Oneness. There has never been any separation in the One, and there never will be, since there is only One. *Being the One Mind* that you are, you will *be whole* Minded and *be whole*; instead of thinking with your physical, limited mind. As you do unto others, you do unto God and your Self as well, by *being One*, so *be whole* and *be service now*. God establishes the template for your magnitude, worthiness, value, perfection, and power *being I Am; so be worthy, be whole,* and *be empowered*. Even more, as you forgive everyone for everything automatically, you will *be whole* and feel whole. *Being whole, being love,* and being holy you will practice gratitude and joy in recognition of your great worth and Truth. Finally, being the fullness of all possibilities because you were born, you are

---

[31] A Course in Miracles (Foundation For Inner Peace, 1975, 1985, 1992), T-6.C.2:8

one of a kind, you are enough, you are perfect just as you are, and you matter, you will realize your Self to *be whole*, be complete, be enough, be worthy, *be beauty, be One,* and be extraordinary as the magnificent person I intend for you to *be now*.

43. Be Equal. Blessed are you to *be equal* as the Father's One Son. You are within me as I Am and your Self, *being equal*. My example of love and forgiveness is to demonstrate who you can *be* also, being created in God's likeness by *being the Christ* temple. Your Truth and reality is Spirit, *being the light* and radiance of the Father. Indeed, my message is for all as One, *being equal*, because the Father has no favorites. I Am for everyone and so should you *be, being love* even for your adversaries and those who don't love God. Even more, *be generous* with all, because there is no separation or preference in the One. Indeed, the law of Oneness verifies all to *be equal* as I Am, so *be One* for all. Finally, celebrate your perfect equality now, *being whole, being holy,* and *being beauty now*.

44. Be Free. Blessed are you to *be free* of sin, fear and guilt by *being innocent* and *being Truth*. Freedom comes from your infinite Truth, *being God's Will* and *being God's glory* as your Self. You are not bound by the fear and limitations of the world, because you are the power to *be free*. Indeed, your freedom to choose, do, and *be* what you desire is God's great gift to His beloved. *Being free*, you design your reality by choosing what you intentionally think. So *be gratitude* for everything, even the undesirable, because creation will adapt to your good thoughts and deliver only good things. You may also *be free* from your past by God's grace, and *be free* from judgment and guilt by *being true forgiveness*. *Being authentic* as your real Self, feeling your feelings, and being

Spirituality For The Common Man

true to who you are, you will *be free* from resistance and separation to be these New Beatitudes now.

45. Be Faith. Blessed are you to *be faith* by being connected to God in your One Mind and heart, *being One*. You may also *be faith* by being in a close relationship with Him. *Being faith* is *being One* with God by being in, by, for, through, and with I Am as your Self. *Being faith, being prayerful, being still, being surrender, being allowing* and *being aligned* are the ways to focus upon and strengthen your connection with God, so *be I Am* and *be faith*. *Being the Christ* temple and embodiment of faith your Self, you will be divine and human in one body. So, follow my example and be a stable influence in this upside down world, being divine while still flesh and bones. This is the human experience that punctuates *being I Am* that, I Am, or God within flesh, rather than just speaking of it. *Being the Christ* Temple embodiment of divine love and forgiveness gives you evidence that I Am for you, since I ask no more of you than I experienced my Self. Herein, may you *be allowing* of your human experiences to remind you of your divine potential and these sacred moments to *be faith* in God. Even more, *be faith* in my keeping power that moves mountains into the sea, because you are the power to *be*. Surely, you are within me as I Am, *being One* soul, *being One* Mind, *being One* Thought, *being One* word, and *being One* life. *Being faith* is *being ho*pe as well, because it is from your mind and heart and not the ego. So show your faith by your confident actions, demonstrating and being what you believe. Beloved, *be faith* and do not doubt or be moved no matter what may come. Even more, may your faith inspire you to be mature and abstain from childish behavior, since *being faith* is *being victorious*. Verily, you may be a resolute master who chooses to transform trials into triumphs, vices into victories, and faintness into faith. Certainly, the Father is more powerful than anything in the world, He is still in control, and through Him all things are possible, so *be One* and *be faith.*

46. Be Detached. Blessed are you to *be detached* from things outside yourself, because you are holy and complete within your Self. The ego thinks you need external things to be complete, but completion comes from what is within. Co-dependency and attachments to things and people are of the illusionary, physical world, so they are not real. Furthermore, *be detached* from judgment, blame, guilt, and reaction. Instead, *be forgiveness,* be the observer, be responsive, *be discipline,* and *be self-control.* Surely, your true happiness is inherent within your Self, being the wholeness, worthiness, and Oneness that you are eternally as I Am. Thus, you will overcome the ego and let go of your attachments and give them nothing to be connected to. Furthermore, *be surrender* and *be allowing* of all to *be now,* and let go of your way for the way to *be.* Verily, there is nothing you need, *being God's Will, being God's Glory,* and *being I Am that, I Am now.*

47. Be Transformed. Blessed are you to choose to *be transformed* and changed by Christ's triumph and Truth of being now. Transformation comes through being, living, experiencing, seeing, loving, forgiving, sharing, accepting, surrendering, aligning, and resurrecting with me. *So, be allowing* of me to be your closest friend and confidant, and rest assured that change is the way for things to get better. Then watch and see what the Lord will do and never be the same again! Now is the time to be self-acceptance, be new, *be resurrected,* and *be renunciation* of sin and fear by changing your perspective. You will also *be transformed* as you realize your divine connection to God, the Holy Spirit, and me, by *being faith.* See your Self and all humankind in holy vision, *being eternal, being innocent,* and *being equal.* Even more, *be the Christ* temple who is love embodied, being the divine within flesh, Mind, heart, words, thoughts, actions, feelings, and being. Lastly, your grandest truth is to *be transformed* by letting grievances go to *be love, be forgiveness,* and *be the light now* as I Am.

48. Be Discipline. Blessed are you *be discipline* by training your mind to think only loving thoughts. Discipline is necessary to control your mind. Since you think both intentional and unintentional thoughts, you must *be discipline* to manifest what you desire. Discipline also rewards you with maturity, wisdom, power, and knowledge, because it allows you to overcome the ego. Surely, you must be able to control your mind to control your life. So, *be present, be aware, be responsible,* monitor, and cancel out all negative ideas immediately so they do not manifest. Your disciplined will aligns your thoughts with mine in every now moment, allowing you to *be God's Will* and *be the One Mind. Being discipline* is the way to follow through and transform your desires into achievement and success. Howbeit, discipline grants you stillness and serenity, responses rather than reactions, order and energy, and self-review and non-judgment. Lastly, *be discipline* and *be directed by the Holy Spirit* in practicing good character, beneficial habits, self- control, stillness, and forgiveness in every opportunity to *be now.*

49. Be Peace. Blessed are you to *be peace* by *being forgiveness* automatically for everyone and everything, every time. Peace begins within your Self and it has no goal other than to *be.* You must *be intentional choice* to *be peace* first, before you can give it away. Indeed, you will *be peace* as you intend to *be the Golden Rule* and *be respectful of all life,* by honoring all souls as One. Even more, being emotionally focused and balanced you will *be peace* as I Am. Your emotions will always reveal your authentic feelings, being your dependable truth gauge. They will continually guide

If You Love and Forgive

you to me, your innermost being, and the right thing to do because when you feel good you are aligned with love and on the right track. And when you don't feel good, you are not aligned with love and what you really desire. So trust your emotions, since they will always lead you home. Herein, being a conduit that is always *being love* and *being peace*, you will shift your energy and the world's energy patterns, just by being your Self. So you can change the world, beloved! Finally, world peace begins within the hearts of every common man and woman as they desire to *be love* and *be forgiveness* now.

Chapter 6

You Are Already Deserving

Accepting your Self to *be God's Child* will change your life, if you so desire to *be*. *Being an extension of God* you are the Father's infinite glory as your Self. Formed in His likeness, your being, nature, and character are what the Father is, so *be* it.

You are the Christ Child who is One of the One, so you are already deserving of all that is. You are also the Christ temple, who embodies The New Beatitudes as your holy Self. In fact, you are so glorious that your Oneness precludes anything other than perfection!

Being holy, being whole, and *being equal* you will see that your deepest longings are already fulfilled. For you are holy, whole, and equal as I Am. And so is everyone else, being all of God's creations. Seeing with holy vision, you find your holiest desires within your soul. Herein are the answers to your questions and your personal peace, worth, and joy. Now you see there is only God and the Christ, and nothing else to desire.

Holy vision is true perception, which sees Spirit rather than the body and all beings as eternal, innocent, and holy. There is no sin, because all creation remains sinless and guiltless as originally created by the Father. Gratefully, the Father continues to see your Self rather than your constructions in the world. Indeed, you remain innocent in true perception, knowledge, and holy vision, *being I Am*.

Your true, divine Self is who you remain in Heaven and may be in the physical world, *being I Am, being the Christ*, and *being aligned*. Albeit, you are playing the game of life and earth is the playground for experience, expansion, exploration, expression, and evolution. Since you are eternal Spirit within a physical body having a human experience, your Spirit and soul remain untouched by negativity and therefore holy.

Within these constructs, you will *be awakened* and *be remembrance* of your true identity, which is love, and your true purpose, which is to *be love*. In so being, may you *be remembrance* that the interconnection and unity of your human self and your divine Self is the goal of the game and the intention of your birth.

Nonetheless, there recently has been much turmoil in your outer world, as Mother Earth is accelerating into the fifth dimension. Clearly the world has not fulfilled mankind as expected, and enlightenment is being called forth for a better way.

These New Beatitudes are the way of enlightenment now. As you embrace these keys to spirituality as empowerments for being, you will acknowledge your innate power to *be*. Then you will *be* cause for accelerating the magnificent effects of Oneness, love, and forgiveness for all creation and all living beings now.

Everything is in perfect divine order, and God is still One. God is also the only power, so the only real cause of life is love, and so may your effects *be*. Furthermore, your eternal Spirit cannot be harmed by anything in the world, so go with the flow, relax, and enjoy the ride, as it has been said. You are creating your life in this now moment, and you can change anytime by choosing again to *be*.

Being already deserving of your Father's love, your vision is one of inspiration, hope, and fulfillment. And *being love* as cause, the effects of your kind thoughts, words, and actions uplift and bless others. Now you will *be the light* that shines into the darkness, *being the Christ* with your name.

So, *be already deserving* of God's Will and glory by being these New Beatitudes now. Beloved, so *be* it.

50. Be Already Deserving. Blessed are you to *be already deserving* as your Father's Child, masterpiece, and extension of His divine Self. *Being One* of the One, you are what your Father is and all that is. God's DNA is the substance of your being, so never think of your Self as any less than perfect, complete, worthy, whole, and being enough. You are already deserving of God's Will and God's glory, *being holy, being eternal,* and *being innocent* as I Am that, I Am now. And so may you *be now*.

51. Be Guided. Blessed are you to *be guided* by Christ's Presence as your Self. For I have said, "Ask and it shall be given." *Being the One Mind* that you are, you will *be guided,* connected, and *be aligned* with me through intuition, inspiration, insight, whispers, signs, signals, visions, synchronicity, and coincidences. So *be free,* resolute, and worry no more, while allowing divine love to order your affairs. *Be intentional choice* and ask to *be directed by the Holy Spirit, being confident* that you will *be guided* in the way to *be*. Beloved, *be still* and know that your desire has already been given, for you have asked and will receive now. So *be* it!

52. Be Infinite. Blessed are you to *be infinite* in your expansiveness of love. God is far more magnificent than this world and its beliefs. The Father's expansive, invincible potential is who you are, since you are His infinite Son and infinite intelligence. So shine your light by being more love and serve those less fortunate than you. Even the least among you is infinite in their creative power to dream, imagine anything they desire, and accomplish bold things. So do not be limited by past conditioning and illusions of separation. Instead, dream big and *be allow*ing of your dreams to manifest, because if you can dream it you can intentionally create it and *be* it! More so, be your infinite destiny and merge your humanity with your divinity to *be the Christ* temple that you are born to *be*. Be the infinite way as well, *being acceptance* of my support, abundance, and Truth that you may *be*. Lastly, *be infinite* in the magnificence of your Self and realize that each day is a gift of new life filled with limitless possibilities to *be resurrection, be the miracle, be the light,* and *be now*.

53. Be Beauty. Blessed are you to *be beauty, be whole,* and *be One* as I Am. Beloved, you are beautiful and perfect just the way you are, *being One* of a kind. All beauty reflects the light of the One who created it, being the innermost light of the Father. Envision the beauty of nature as a window into the essence of God. Find joy in the bird's song, the flower's perfume, the light that surrounds you, and the Presence of your holy Self that is the beauty, perfection, and magnificence of God. Finally, *be remembrance* that true beauty is within all, being all that is as innocence, love, compassion, understanding, acceptance, Oneness, and confidence from the Father who is All.

54. Be Confident. Blessed are you to *be confident, being an extension of God* as His beloved Child. You are already deserving, *being holy, being whole,* and *being eternal.* Indeed, confidence is not egotistical, but the ability to *be truth* and *be integrity* even if you are afraid. Whatever scares you, do it anyway, being sure that your fears are false evidence appearing real, as it has been said. So, be sure that in *being love* you are empowered and capable, and in *being joy* you are strengthened and confident, because love is the greatest power of all. Acknowledge your good that triumphs all fear and illusion, and every small or great success, because I Am with you and for you. Surround yourself with a great support team and *be confident* in your eternal relationship and partnership with me, trusting I Am to order your affairs and well-being now. *Being faith* especially in the eternal Truth that you are, and your close relationship with me, you must *be confident.* You may certainly *be confident* that all of God's promises are true, you are not alone, and life is eternal. As Oprah Winfrey says, she is "confident knowing she is supported by a power greater than herself," and she is! Finally, *being confident* that you are these New Beatitudes your Self, you will *be I Am* that, I Am now.

55. Be Wisdom. Blessed are you to *be wisdom* as your Christ Self. Wisdom is more than knowledge of God's Will; it is *being willing* to *be God's Will. Being wisdom,* you discern and realize the Father's Will to be your divine Truth, highest good, and greatest joy. Wisdom beholds the innocence of everyone in holy vision as well, so you may truly see. You are completely supported by God's Will, which is happening for you, not to you. It is also wise to realize that the physical world and its illusions aren't real. *Being in the world but not of the world*, you must live with illusions, being not of them. Yet you may *be intentional choice* as to why illusions exist and what you may learn from them, and don't give illusions power over you. As you believe it will be done unto you, so *be wisdom* and *be detached* from temporary illusions and expected outcomes. *Be intentional creation* in your desire to give meaning to God's real creations, and positively choose how you desire to respond and feel now. It is always a great choice to *be forgiveness* and *be intentional thought* in response to illusions. Because the choice is always love or fear. Even more, *being wisdom* assures your promotion after trials, since it grants a greater appreciation of life and knowledge. Surely, wisdom is given to those who possess an attainable mission greater than themselves, for the betterment of all, so be mature and *be wisdom* now.

56. Be Balance. Blessed are you to *be balance* by being your divine Self and human self as One. May you also *be equal* with everyone as One, *being One*. The law of cause and effect balances every action with another, so you will reap as you have sown. You may balance the masculine and feminine aspects of your Self as well, pairing one with another equally. May you *be balanced* emotionally as well when a loved one passes, because Spirit is eternal and you will see everyone again, even your beloved pets. It is good to balance your work and rest time, as well as your service and solitude. Furthermore, may you balance your higher, divine Self and lower, shadow self, since each one teaches you contrast. Honor your shadow, acknowledge it, forgive it, and allow it to be recognized, so the lessons you learned will not repeated. May you balance your decisions with prayer, giving equal thought to both as well. And if you withdraw and fast for insight, may you also balance that time with celebration and enthusiasm. Lastly, *be remembrance* that life is balanced by birth and death, and you have experienced both many times.

57. Be Hope. Blessed are you to *be hope* and *be trust* in God. Hope views all with holy vision, seeing beyond the physical to the Spirit within. The ego makes you think you can fail but you cannot be unsuccessful; surely failure is an opportunity to try again and you will always succeed if you don't give up. So *be hope* that all of God's promises are true, because they are. More so, speak truth to power, *be hope* in the midst of change, and keep your sense of humor, because things will always get better. Finally, *be faith, be courage, be hope* in your Self, *be hope* in me, and never give up hope, because hope is eternal.

Chapter 7

Why You Will See With My Eyes

Now you will see with my eyes in holy vision, as you realize the Truth of life. No more sad illusions shade the glory of I Am, or the promise of holiness. Thus, there is only Oneness, Truth, and innocence for all Creation, as you look beneath the body to witness the indwelling Spirit.

I always behold the face of Christ in all my brothers and sisters, because there is only One. Holy vision sees the Truth that returns you to your Father, exchanging misperception with true perception, fear with love, guilt with innocence, judgment with forgiveness, sickness with healing, sadness with joy, separation with Oneness, and illusion with reality.

God is the great Creator, and as an extension of Him so are you. Oneness is knowledge and Truth, which is God's creative Thought. Being your Self you will *be aligned* with God's Thought, which is *being the One Mind* that you are. Or you may *be aligned* with the ego, thinking separately and fearfully yourself. Beloved, everything began with a thought of some kind, so *be One, be Truth, be intentional creation*, and *be intentional Thought*.

You have created your life by your intentional and unintentional thoughts, words, and actions. Everything that you think, say, and do creates, because everything is energy and energy creates. The New Beatitudes are keys to increasing your energy frequency and vibration, and thus your love, joy, peace, and well-being.

Fearful, negative behaviors such as shame, guilt, fear and anger directly correlate with low consciousness levels and this energy vibrates slowly. As you change your frequency and correlating consciousness from negative to positive, you will *be empowered, be love, be joy, be healed, be peace*, and *be enlightened*. These positive energy frequencies vibrate quicker and allow you to feel better and accomplish more. Since life is energy frequency and vibration, being The New Beatitudes is the way to *be!*

In fact, as you think you will be, since you create your life with your thoughts. It may be noted that you think over sixty thousand thoughts a day, and many of them are repetitive. Just imagine the power of all those thoughts and the energy you are projecting. If over half of those thoughts are real, loving, and joyous, you will *be remembrance* of your Self being these New Beatitudes. You will also create your best life now.

If on the other hand, your thoughts are fearful and negative, you would do well to monitor what you are thinking and cancel out anything you do not desire to *be*. If an unwanted thought appears, recognize it and delete it by thinking something positive and better in its place, or what you actually desire to experience. In this way you are *being intentional creation*, which is surely the way to *be*.

More explicitly, The New Beatitudes are the way to *be intentional creation*. Intention is the great creative force that is the power of God as your Self. Your intention is profoundly important since what you intend or desire will manifest. *Being intentional creation* is living deliberately and being purposeful in your thoughts, words, actions and feelings. This is your Self-fulfilling prophecy, beloved, so *be* it!

It is important to note that your feelings intensify your creations, since they are the passion of your desires. Your desires are the deepest longings of your Father, or Sire, residing within you as your Self. Feeling something passionately and intensely allows you to experience and express it quickly. Keep this in mind as you desire for your manifestations to appear, since they will not come before the intention, allowing, and alignment of the energy that created them.

God shares His powers of creation with you by appointing you the Creator of your life. Being in the world you create by using the law of cause and effect. As you intentionally choose love to be the cause of your manifestations, the effects will *be the miracle*. You may also *be the miracle* as you join your Mind with others intentionally for the healing and blessing of all, *being One*.

You may also use the law of attraction, which states that like energy attracts itself. Or, your energy, frequency, vibrations, thoughts and feelings draw more of the same to you by their matching vibrational alignment, so *be aligned* and *be One*.

In fact, everything is energy so your thoughts and emotions vibrate with energy. As I have said, positive thoughts vibrate at high frequencies so they attract order, joy, and well-being. On the other hand, negative thoughts vibrate at low frequencies so they attract disorder, negativity, and uncertainty.

As you intend to *be love*, divine power, guidance, and synchronicity combine to bless you with an abundance of your desired necessities as well as the joy and peace that you have always dreamed of.

Even more, *being intentional creation, being love,* and *being joy* will uplift everyone to a higher vibrational frequency, contributing to the healing of mankind and the collective consciousness of the planet! Beloved, since all Minds are joined, *being love* is the way to uplift mankind, heal all creation, and change the world, so *be love now!*

Actually, thoughts are solid things that are impressed upon the etheric energy waves of your soul, where they are a record of the choices that you made during each lifetime. If they are not cancelled out immediately and allowed to remain, they will be fully expressed in your reality, and in the etheric sea, *being eternal.*

They are also stored in the Akashic records, where they are looked upon by all as a permanent accounting of your beliefs, thoughts and choices. This documentation will either *be Heaven on Earth,* or something less as you recall this lifetime later from another dimension.

It is important to note that the collective consciousness of Mother Earth is an example of creation, being the combined thoughts of all living beings, including the fearful and negative ideas that mankind would not desire to manifest, and this is how natural disasters occur.

So, I ask you now to imagine how things would change for the better if everyone understood this and created intentionally. In so being, a good way to manifest your Thoughts is to use the phrase I Am. Just Think or say:

" I Am_____now. So *be* it."

You may add what you desire in the blank space, phrasing it in the present tense.

Creating with the phrase "I Am" orders your desires to be granted, because you acknowledge your Self to *be an extension of God*. God creates with the phrase "I Am," so *be remembrance* that the words you think or speak following "I Am" create your life. Always be positive and declare what you are and will *be* intentionally. Completing your Thought with the words "now" and "so *be* it" manifests it immediately, because I Am is manifesting it now as your Self.

In so being, the only answer you can possibly receive from God is "so *be* it." You may use this exercise whenever you are *being intentional creation* and *being intentional Thought*. So *be* it!

A good mental exercise is to visualize your desires manifesting as if they already have. While visualizing, imagine the specific details of your desires and *be joy* in their realization. When you have completed your envisioned dream come true, *be surrender* and give it to God, and so will it *be!*

Verily, you will also desire to *be intentional choice*, which is deliberately choosing what you desire to manifest. Every day you make up to five thousand choices, so *be intentional choice* in who you choose to *be*.

Being the Christ you will intentionally see with my eyes and be these New Beatitudes now. Beloved, so *be* it.

58. Be Responsible. Blessed are you to *be responsible* for your creations, realizing that what you do to another you do to God and your Self. So, do not blame others for what you are experiencing, because you are 100% accountable for your life, thoughts, choices, actions, and feelings. May you also *be responsible* for your own healing by *being unconditional forgiveness*. May you *be responsible* for what you see as well; if change is called for *be intentional choice*, embrace a new perspective, and be holy vision. Even more, *be responsible* for your resistance and fear, since you called in the lessons for what you must address and overcome. Surely, false evidence is not real and perfect love casts out fear, so *be courage*, be fearless, and *be victory*. It is also good to *be responsible* for your thoughts and choices, since actions follow thought. Additionally, *being responsible* for your thoughts, words, actions, and feelings is the way to *be love* without grievances and judgment now. And finally, *be responsible* and accountable for yourself and your soul, knowing yourself and being true to your Self. For as Shakespeare wisely said, "to thine own Self be true."

59. Be Aware. Blessed are you to *be aware* of the Truth of your being, and the divinity, innocence, and love that you are. May you additionally *be aware* of God's voice, your Spirituality, your Spirit's longing to align yourself with your divine Self, how well you are playing the game of life, how well you are *being love*, how well you are *being forgiveness*, and how well you are *being service*. It is also good to *be aware* of what you are learning and the wisdom of the lessons, to *be aware* of your joy and inspiration of others, and what you are giving back to mankind. May you *be aware* of your eternal energy, intentions, consciousness, allowing, and alignment as well, *being mindful* of your energetic point of attraction. Likewise, may you *be mindful* of the Oneness of Creation and the equality of all souls, by *being respectful of all life*. Similarly, *being aware* of your judgments you will *be non-judgment* and *be love* without grievances, and *being* aware of the ego's illusions you will *be directed by the Holy Spirit* in *being unconditional forgiveness*. It is equally good to *be aware* of unconscious egotistical roles, by *being detached, being non- judgment,* and *being the miracle* in the present moment. Albeit, may you *be aware* or your feelings and energetic vibrations as well, by focusing on your greatest joy, happiest thoughts, and grandest creations. Surely, *being surrender* of everything to me for the highest good of all, furthers your awareness of the greatest good to *be now*. And finally, *be aware* of how many lives you changed, uplifted, and blessed, being these New Beatitudes now.

60. Be Aligned. Blessed are you to *be aligned* with your higher Self, soul, or God in you. *Being aligned* by merging your human self with your divine Self is fulfilling your soul's purpose. And very importantly, your desired manifestations are realized when you are vibrationally aligned with God by *being love*. This is true since you are vibrational beings and like attracts like. While *being aligned* you will *be joy, be empowered, be well-being,* be positive, and feel great, since alignment is your power. When you disregard your connection to God you will not feel or be well. Feeling negative and unhappy is the ego's trick, to make you feel less and be less. Yet, alignment accelerates the energy of your creations exponentially and assures your success. So, focus on what you desire to create, and pay attention only to that. I say this because if you "want" something you will stay in a place of wanting it as long as you feel that way. Rather, think and say the words desire, like, and have when intentionally creating, while *being aligned*. *Being aligned* you will also do for others before yourself, desire nothing, and be fulfilled by Spirit. May you *be aligned* with beauty, nature, and the present, now moment that represents the infinite Self within, *being I Am*. Even more, may you be a master of alignment and always *be aware* of your creations by *being love*. At the end of the day, it is your thought, choice, and power to *be aligned* with I Am as your Self, since you are a creator, creating matter, and so may you *be!*

61. Be Intentional Creation. Blessed are you to be co-creative and partners with God by *being intentional creation*. Thought creates form, so the key to intentional creation is vibrational alignment. Actually, *being One* your Self, you create with God so you create your life. Through your vibrational attunement, you attract and magnetize to your Self what you desire, so *be love* and *be aligned*. Your intention is very important and what matters most, as it is reflected in your creations. Creation is also a basic, essential desire, and you are here to create yourself in the ways of love and forgiveness. Love is your power to create and your freedom to choose and *be*. Creative Mind receives your thought and creates, since all thought manifests in some way. Being in partnership with God allows God's Will to be done and you to be a creator. *So, be intentional creation* by focusing and aligning with love as cause for all your creations, and the effects will be miraculous. Finally, observe your power and *be intentional choice* to change your mind and see with holy vision, so you will be your divine potential and create your best life now.

62. Be Present. Blessed are you to *be present* and be mindful in this now moment. *Being now* in the present moment you may be attuned to Spirit as Spirit; so you will just *be!* Spirit is perfect as it is, so you may just *be;* you do not have to do anything. Likewise, *being present* you will *be love* without judgment in every thought, word, action, and feeling. May you also be observant for every opportunity to *be forgiveness* in all ways, *being vigilant* for God and Truth. Herein, thousands of minds will *be aligned* by your present and constant devotion to God. *Being present* you may be certain that I Am with you as well, since God is within you, and you are within God, *being One*. May you also *be present* in the bliss and blessing of every ordinary moment that you live and breathe. Lastly, get out of your own way and be dependent on God, being dedicated to *being now* in every present moment as I Am.

63. Be Intentional Breath. Blessed are you to *be intentional breath*, be quiet, *be still*, meditate, and rest your mind. Although you are eternal Spirit and not a physical body, it is good to quiet yourself by breathing deeply. Your breath is an innate calming tool that soothes you anytime and anywhere, so inhale and exhale deliberately. Your breath is also great and powerful, being the first and last thing you do in life. Beloved, *be present* in the silence and space between each breath which is God, play the game of life joyfully, dance to your own music, be within God as I Am, and *be abiding* with me now.

64. Be Intentional Thought. Blessed are you to *be intentional Thought* by *being love* and always choosing love instead of fear. Thought with a capital "T" is of the Father and His gift unto you. So pay attention to the real, loving Thoughts you desire to create and feel, and cancel out the rest. As Louise Hay says, if you can fathom how powerful your thoughts are, you will only think positive thoughts and heal your life. She says that practicing positive affirmations is a powerful way to create the new, fulfilling life that you deserve. So be positive Minded and never allow another negative thought to remain. You may also look at your fears and *be willing* to let them go to *be forgiveness* completely. Even more, it is good to *be remembrance* that thought is vibration, so Think intentionally and create your reality by focusing on love, joy, and alignment. Visualize and feel your Thoughts manifesting, since what you focus upon for fifty-one percent of the time manifests. Feel what you desire and resonate with it, *being joy* and being attuned with it, and it will *be now*. Surely, intentional creation is a matching game; match your vibration, resonation, and alignment with that which you desire and it will *be* realized now. This is another way of saying, "The Kingdom of God is within you." For I have said, ask and it shall be given, seek and you shall find, and knock and it shall be opened. Indeed, it is God's Will and great joy to give good things those who Think intentionally and ask. So *be* it.

65. Be Intentional Choice. Blessed are you to *be intentional choice* by choosing love rather than fear. Realize there is only one decision, and that is for God and Truth. Your power to decide is miraculous. Creation, new life, and holy vision extend intention as you see Christ within everyone, everywhere. I have said there are two thought systems and only two emotions, love and fear. What's not love is a call for love, so be intentional choice to *be love* and *be forgiveness*, and *be gratitude* for the opportunity to *be* once again. You may also choose to *be joy* by training your mind, focusing on what feels good, and *being salvation* which is your true calling. *Be remembrance* that when there is a choice to make, you don't have to be right, just *be love!* Lastly, *be remembrance, be present, be self-control, be intentional choice* to respond rather than react, and monitor the words you think, choose, and say after "I Am," because they create your reality. It is also good to watch, observe, and choose the way to *be* as well. Even more, be intentional speech by *being confident* and finding your voice, speaking your Truth, being positive and uplifting others or being quiet. Verily, words convey the energy of life and death, so if you can't say something nice, don't say anything at all. So *be* it.

66. Be Practice. Blessed are you to *be practice* in being these New Beatitudes now. *Being God's Will* as your will takes constant, intentional practice. Train your mind to focus on love and joy consistently, so the powerful law of attraction will magnetize more love and joy to you. May you also practice *being gratitude* so the blocks to your Self-actualization will be removed easily by forgiveness. Beloved, *be now*, be new, be child-like, and be born again in every now moment you choose to *be*. Lastly, you may practice the Unconditional Forgiveness Thought whenever you judge another or yourself, so your joy will increase and you will thrive.

Chapter 8

What You Will See With My Eyes

Seeing with my eyes in holy vision is a new way to look at life. It is a fresh outlook that sees true reality beyond the world's beliefs. The world sees sin, guilt, and death; but holy vision only beholds innocence, holiness, and eternal life for One and all.

I hope you have chosen to *be now*, so you are not at the mercy of the world and the ego anymore. *Being the light*, you will *be the way* so that others may remember who they are by your example. And being your Self you will lovingly serve another who has forgotten their holiness and glory, reminding them to *be now*.

Through holy vision the blinders have been removed from your eyes, allowing you to see beyond the veil into other dimensions. Many of you are now thinking out of the box, as you say in your modern language, pushing the limits in remembrance of the unseen.

You realize your three dimensional life is the experience of separation and defense. Having experienced enough of this, you desire something more. So, you are expanding your Self into the fourth dimension, which is the awareness of limitless understanding and imagination. This is the dimension that you access when you meditate and retrieve information from other realms.

Even more, the fifth dimension is being desired in the awareness of expanded evolution, and many brothers and sisters are experiencing this now. The fifth dimension is out of this world, since it is where you actually remember who you are and *be* it now.

The new reality that you desire is the way of your divine Self and Spirit, and it will not be forgotten any longer. Holy vision honors I Am who has called all to rise up and *be now*. Knowing all that has been concealed by the illusions of the world, you desire change so you may resonate within the higher vibrations of love, joy, healing, peace, and enlightenment.

Specifically, *being love* you will experience increased joy and appreciation, enhanced well-being, deeper surrender, allowing, and alignment, improved health, closer relationships, greater work satisfaction, and a more positive attitude. You will also honestly love and forgive everyone and everything, *being the Christ* temple as your Self.

Likewise, Dr. David Hawkins, in his brilliant book *Power vs. Force*, studied human consciousness and created a scale to map out why people behave like they do. The consciousness levels are divided into positive and negative groups, with love, joy, healing, peace, and enlightenment being the top positive levels. It is interesting to note that one person vibrating at 500 or the level of love positively uplifts 750,000 people. A person at 600 or the level of peace uplifts 10 million people, and someone at the level of 700 to 1000, which is enlightenment, uplifts 70 million people! So you can change the world by *being love, being joy* and *being healed,* (which are both level 540), *being peace,* and *being enlightenment* and this is why being The New Beatitudes is so important for humanity now!

Look at the difference just one individual can make with an elevated consciousness, and imagine how much better life on earth will *be* when thousands and hopefully millions of people are consciously aware of their alignment, frequency, and vibration. A Oneness consciousness is possible and life can *be Heaven on Earth* by *being love, being joy, being healed, being peace,* and *being enlightened.* The New Beatitudes are the way to *be, be-*cause they are the keys to improving and elevating life!

Beloved, be the cause of love by *being love* and *be* the change that is so urgently desired at this time, and the effects will *be the miracle* that uplift and heal mankind. So *be* it now.

The following New Beatitudes are what you will see with my eyes in holy vision now. Beloved, so *be* it.

67. Be Trust. Blessed are you to *be trust* in God rather than man. Surely, I Am is more powerful than anything in the world, so *be trust* and be dependent upon God. Be committed and *be trust* in God's Will, no matter what, and avoid taking the easy way out. For herein lies your integrity and victory. May you *be faith* as well, realizing there are no challenges or worries that you cannot overcome, since challenges imply doubt, and trust in God makes doubt impossible.[32] I Am abundant life, power, protection, and strength, so *be trust* in me as your constant companion, focus on my presence, and watch what I do on your behalf. Howbeit, may you *be trust* in your Self, because you already have, know, and are all that you need, being all that is as I Am. So release all worry and concern, relax, be relief, go with the flow, *be blessed*, and *be trust* in me to guide you and keep you, because I will never forsake you.

68. Be Intuition. Blessed are you to *be intuition* and acknowledge the still, small voice within that is the Holy Spirit. He is your inner guide and true expression of your divine Self, that is my Self and God's Self. Intuition is solid evidence of your Presence within God as well, since it is an internal GPS system that guides you in the most direct route to your highest good. Verily, your intuition is your soul's connection, communication, and internal voice, so listen, be focused, value, and acknowledge the truth being shared. *Being intuition* and being instinctual will save you much needless effort, because it is what you desire to know at just the right time. Paying attention and listening to your intuition when prompted by God toward action, no matter what the request, will bless and guide you in miraculous, supernatural ways. So *be intuition* and *be directed by the Holy Spirit* in creating your best life now.

69. Be Integrity. Blessed are you to *be integrity* by resembling God's character your Self. Clearly, integrity is *being love* without holding grudges and *being forgiveness* automatically, rather than judging automatically. It is also doing what you say you will do, when you say you will do it, and always being your best. So strive for excellence,

---

[32] A Course in Miracles (Foundation For Inner Peace, 1975, 1985, 1992), M-4.II.2:6

virtue, character, and wisdom, and *be the light* unto the darkness. Hold your Truth sacred and *be respectful* of your beliefs and all life. Similarly, may your words *be aligned* with your thoughts as you follow through and initiate action that represents, serves, and is the proof of a life well lived. Lastly, my character is one of Truth, holiness, love, Oneness, honesty, boldness, integrity, gentleness, and joy, and so may you *be*.

70. Be Understanding. Blessed are you to *be understanding* that God is the only power and He created you; you did not create yourself. Your presence is from God, your life is a miracle, and you are a masterpiece designed by the grand designer of all life. Therefore, you are amazing, holy, beautiful, and phenomenal! *Being understanding* of Truth, may you *be practice*, magnetize, and attract more opportunities to *be now*. Even more, may you *be understanding* of your brothers and sisters to *be innocent*, beholding all in holy vision. May you *be understanding* of Oneness as well, by doing unto others as you would God and your Self. Since, everyone desires to *be loved*, understood, validated, and valued. May you also *be understanding* of the power of love, by listening with gentleness, *being compassion*, and *being the miracle*. All the more, may you *be understanding* of your innate worthiness, power, inspiration, imagination, and creativity that express Christ as your Self. Lastly, *be understanding* of the power of forgiveness, so you will finally *be joy*, *be peace*, and *be healed* as I Am.

71. Be Passion. Blessed are you to *be passion* in your desire and purpose to *be now*. Realizing who you are, *being God's Child*, what you are, which is love, and why you are here now, which is to *be love* and *be forgiveness*, you will *be passion* in your desire to *be*. Thus, your passion mirrors your divine purpose by allowing you to reflect and create your version of the Christ that you are. Therefore, you may *be passion* in your work by following your heart and doing what makes you sing, doing what you love, what you must do, what you are called to do by your inner voice and the Holy Spirit, and what is necessary, uncommon, and radical. Beloved, *be passion* while playing as well, celebrating this time to *be joy*, be fun, *be the light*, and *be the miracle*. More so, *be courage*, be bold, dream big, and dream now! Be attentive to your feelings of expectation; *being allowing* and *being aligned* with your innate calling that will not be ignored. Be sure that God supports you and the universe is for you. Remain steadfast as providence arranges supernatural provision in unexpected, miraculous, daring ways. Verily, may you *be passion* for God by loving Him as your Source and Creator, and His divinity that He extends and includes you as the beloved. Finally, *be trust, be discipline, be endurance, be still, be passion*, never give up, and always listen to God's innate voice that calls you to your predestined, glorious destiny now.

72. Be Imagination. Blessed are you to *be imagination* which is inspiration from God, divine Thought, and creativity. God is a creator and so are you. So, create your greatest dreams come true by imagining them as reality now. Be curious and playful within the many different realms because it is fun and beneficial; for it is through imagination that shape takes form. Imagine your grandest dreams being fulfilled, since through your imagination, vision, faith, and alignment it will *be*. Play the game of life with an adventurous spirit, by expressing wonder and celebrating often. For surely, my nature is wondrous and joyous and so may you *be*. Actually, wonder amplifies imagination by combining your magnetized, contrasting experiences in the best way possible for your greatest good and self-definition. Finally, imagine, envision, and focus on world peace and the salvation of mankind, as the common man desires to *be God's Will* now.

73. Be in the World but not of the World. Blessed are you to overcome the ego and the world, by *being in the world but not of the world.* The holy scriptures state that you are in the world, but ask you to be not of the world. So *be renunciation* and relinquish the world's opinion of you to be your higher, holy Self now. The world consists of man's limited ego-based perceptions of sin, fear, and death. As I have stated, this shared perception is actually illusion, because the only true reality is in Heaven. Having faith, keeping the faith, and *being faith* is the way to be not of the world. The world will not believe the Truth and reality of your being, and that is okay. Just *be not of the world* by being these New Beatitudes, because you are meant to *be* your divine Self now.

Part Three

MAKE THIS LIFETIME COUNT

Chapter 9

How to Achieve Closeness to Me

You will make this lifetime count by being in a close, personal relationship with me. And this is the best thing you can ever do for yourself. Being close to me you will *be remembrance* of your Self as Spirit and God's beloved Child created in His image, and not the littleness the world has impressed upon you. The world's fear based thought system is the opposite of your Truth and my love based thought system that clarifies your magnificence, perfection, and Oneness with God, the Holy Spirit, all creation, and me.

So, be close to me simply by desiring my presence, and realizing I Am here with you now and always will be. Call on me, call out my name, think thoughts of me, spend time with me, share your desires and needs with me, and realize that I know you as my Self. Being sure that I love you and care about your concerns, and provide for you abundantly, you see that our time together enriches your Self-awareness, assures you that you are not alone, reminds you that I Am with you and for you, and verifies your potential is *to be the Christ* with your name. So acknowledge me, *be love for me, be One* with me and All that is, and you will *be guided* and directed in the way to enjoy Christ in you as your Self.

Verily, *being loved by me* you will realize your Self to be within my Self as One. Remembering who you really are, you will know that we have always been together as One and we still are One. This is why I have said "I will never leave you or forsake you," because I can't. Surely, there is no earthly relationship that compares with the Oneness between a soul that loves me and me, for we are truly One.

So when you think of me I know it, because we are connected. I am aware of your every thought, your next breath, your deepest pain, and your greatest dream, because it is also mine. I have known you for all time and through all of your many lifetimes, and we will be together throughout all eternity as One.

Being One is the way to merge yourself with God to be your greatest potential and create you best life now. You may *be* this by being close to me in a relationship, being receptive to me and allowing me to be your closest friend, indwelling guide, protector, and teacher. You will *be intuition* as well, wherein you hear my still, small voice directing you in the way to *be holy, be Truth,* and *be awakened now*. Even more, you will be perfect peace by keeping your mind upon me, for I Am peace.

How to Achieve Closeness to Me

Intentionally *being love* and *being forgiveness* will additionally align our Minds as the One Mind. Similarly, *being prayerful*, meditating, practicing yoga, *being still, being abiding, being surrender, being allowing, being aligned, being open-minded, being guided* and *being intentional breath* with me in the constant moments will also accelerate your intuition.

Furthermore, being close to me you will be a temple of light and love that shines from within, much like a city on a hill. Your inner being of light and love radiates out unto all and is undeniable. Thus you will be certain, *be confident*, be inspiration or in Spirit, *be intentional creation*, and be these New Beatitudes more easily. Thinking upon your holiness and loveliness amplifies your awareness of it, and furthers your being it. So *be* it!

However, you may desire to be close to me because you have been broken by the hurtful ways of the world. Your own personal will has not sustained you, and the pain of your trials has been difficult to bear. Thus, you are looking for support and comfort from One who loves you dearly, and for answers beyond yourself and within your Self, which is where you will find me.

As you overcome your fear and pride and reach out to me, I will be there. My steady eye is always upon you, and my infinite awareness is always within you. Indeed, the more you desire to be close to me, the closer you will be, beloved. And the more you contemplate my presence, being attentive to me and acknowledging me in the moment, the more it becomes you.

So share your thoughts and feelings with me. Talk with me, think with me, abide with me, trust me, *be aligned* with me, be attuned to me, and live your life with me. *Be love for me* and be sure I love you, for I am always watching over you and making a way where there wasn't one.

As you know me you will see my face in every common man and woman, and in all living beings. You will also acknowledge my essence in situations and circumstances that ask the most of you, and bring out the best in you, because I inspire you to *be the Christ* temple and embodiment of The New Beatitudes.

Indeed, the joy of our relationship is out of this world, because we are not confined by the limited thoughts of the ego. Rather, we communicate within our unlimited, true Selves as One life, One Mind, and One Self. So, *be abiding* and *be aligned* with me, by develop a daily practice of prayer and meditation, while *being still* and *being present*. *Be practice* listening to your inner being as well, and you will be given insight and intuition from the Holy Spirit and me that guides you in being your greatest joy and well-being now.

Howbeit, if you witness judgment, fear, or attack thoughts call on me and *be directed by the Holy Spirit* to be more love. As you ask, we guide you in forgiving the illusions and separation of the world, by realizing them to be unreal and nothing. Thus, may you *be remembrance* that only love is real, love is All that is, and unconditional love holds no grievances, so *be love*.

Herein, you might experience inspired Thoughts, ideas, happenings, occurrences in nature, signs, feelings, miracles, and whisperings in the wind or in your ear that are gifts from God. Beloved, no matter how we communicate with you, you will recognize your closest friends and our unconditional love and guidance for you.

Even more, as you are close to me you will make this lifetime count by living a life of purpose. Purpose is found through *being service*, being helpful, and *being sharing* with others beyond yourself. Thus you will *be the One Mind* that you are by intentionally joining, Thinking, and praying for all to *be loved, be blessed*, and *be healed*. It is such a blessing for all life to *be loved by me*, and to be appreciated, cared for, and respected abundantly. This you may do additionally for me, *being the Christ* that you are, with you own words, deeds, hands, and feet. And I thank you, beloved.

Being respectful of all life and *being sacrifice* for the innocents are more paramount ways to serve, for when you save an animal's life it is equivalent to saving a human life in God's eyes, since a soul is a soul. Especially since animals are teachers and disciples of unconditional love and forgiveness and dependent upon mankind for their welfare, they must be honored and *be respected*. So I ask you now, how many lives will you save and how will you be the difference and be the change for our animal friends?

There are many more ways to be significant and evolve your soul for all eternity. For example, you might be purposeful by being more love and doing an unexpected good deed daily, reaching out and forgiving someone or yourself, doing unto others before yourself, uplifting someone every day with a smile or kind word, and living beyond yourself by donating to a charity, volunteering at a hospital, hospice, or SPCA, picking up litter in the road, on the beach, or in the water, holding the door for someone, carrying someone's heavy bags, and the list goes on and on.

Surely, as you shift from fear to love in a holy instant, and practice staying there by actually being the holy instant, you are standing on holy ground. And this is a very good place to be.

Albeit, these New Beatitudes are further ways to be close to me and make this lifetime count. Beloved, so *be* it.

74. Be Surrender. Blessed are you to *be surrender* of your will to *be God's Will*. The common cause for the common man is *being God's Will*, which is *being surrender* of fear and negativity to be Spirit as your higher, holy Self. *Being surrender* of your worldly perspective to be holy vision and see as God sees is *being Truth* as well. This is *being surrender* of the ego to *be love now*. Being surrender is also the way to allow God to be God and manifest your greatest good in the quickest way possible. Verily, surrender multiplies your strength since it replaces your sight with my insight, and your weakness with my power. Surrender is also you power, for when you release your will to *be God's Will* you will *be empowered*. *Being surrender* also releases attachments to the outcome, and allows the Holy Spirit to heal your mind, so *be detached* and *be forgiveness*. Even more, *being surrender* is *being responsible* for your thoughts by allowing me to direct you, so "let go and let God" and trust the process. *Being surrender* also allows me to handle your concerns, while you align, release, and experience relief. May you surrender your guilt and forgive yourself as well, for whatever you are holding onto, because you did the best that you could at the time. Albeit, may you *be surrender* to God's grace, by allowing Spirit to supersede on your behalf. Finally, *being surrender* to *be God's Will* strengthens your belief, improves your behavior, accelerates your becoming, honors your *being*, and enables you to *be the Christ* that you were born to *be now*.

75. Be Willing. Blessed are you to *be willing* and dedicated to *being the way now*. Be holy vision and *be willing* to see love within all as One. *Be willing* to change your mind and perspective, seeing beyond the physical to the One Spirit within all life. *Be willing* to love yourself, and everyone else, because love is the way to *be*. *Be willing* to surrender to your good so you may receive the increase inherent in *being God's Will*. May you also *be willing* to *be directed by the Holy Spirit* in witnessing fear to be unreal, forgiven, and released. *Be willing* to heal your mind and correct your thinking, by *being forgiveness* and *being the miracle*. *Be willing* to *be gratitude* and *be joy* in living this terrific life, and to appreciate your blessings. *Be willing* to end your sense of separation by *being Truth, being One,* and *being respectful of all life*. May you also *be willing* to be close to me and to depend on me as your closest friend, because I Am. Further, *be willing* to *be Heaven on Earth* by being your divine Self, *being the Christ* temple, and being these New Beatitudes now.

76. Be Humble. Blessed are you to *be humble* by *being love for God* and being close to me now. Love is your true reality as I Am, so *be love* and *be humble*. Humility is not meager, but naturally modest in the Oneness of I Am. Humility desires only God and requires nothing as well. In *being humble* you will realize, accept, and be yourself, by *being God's glory*. Likewise, you will *be equal, be One,* and *be service* for all who are God and your Self by *being humble*. You will similarly *be humble* as you realize the grandeur of being authentically empowered, by aligning your personality with your divine Self in the same body. Albeit, true humility thinks of others more than itself, so *be humble*. Beloved, your genius rests in this profound reconciliation and Self-actualization, so *be humble now*.

77. Be Service. *Blessed* are you to *be service* to God by helping all. Giving and receiving are the same,[33] so serve others and the universe will serve you. For surely, giving is the way to receive and understand; it is not the way to lose anything but to gain everything. You already have all the

---
33 A Course in Miracles (Foundation For Inner Peace, 1975, 1985, 1992), W-pII.225.1:1

Spirituality For The Common Man

worthiness and power you could desire within your Self, because nothing is outside of you. And, since your cup runneth over, you may freely give to realize and exemplify what you already have. Thus, I ask you to give and receive generously, and *be service* by doing whatever is needed to make the way easier for another who is God in disguise. You will realize your significance by *being service* for all who are equally One. And since there is only One, what you do for others you do for God and your Self, *being One*. Also, if you wish to feel better and be uplifted, help someone and be the difference in their life. *Be remembrance* that the other is you as well, so serve them as your Self first, and do for them as your Self. And thus you multiply the good effects of your loving cause. Verily, you will *be service, be guided, be the miracle*, be devoted, be significant, be purposeful, *be One, be the Golden Rule*, and receive what you give by being a generous giver to all as One now.

78. Be Sharing. Blessed are you to *be sharing* with others as you would God and your Self. What belongs to you belongs to God and everyone, so do for others and *be sharing*. Withhold what you have and more will not be given unto you. Sharing is also *being confident* of your abundance and knowing that you always have more than you desire. Everything that is shared is multiplied, so *be sharing* by giving much and receiving much, which is a universal Law of God. Do for others before yourself and give to them what you desire, so as to multiply your good intentions, *being sharing*. Another words, create for others first, giving to them and doing for them what you desire for yourself, *being One* and *being sharing*, because there is only One. May you also Think about giving and sharing, like God Thinks, and Source will provide. Furthermore, *be sharing* and be unlimited in your One Mind to imagine everything you desire for all, because if you can Think it, it will *be*. Finally, *being sharing* you will shift from a receiving mentality to a giving mentality. Desire more for others than yourself and be truly wealthy. Desiring to be more sharing, Source desires to share more with you. Indeed, your sharing attitude will transform and inspire all in all ways, so *be sharing*.

79. Be Prayerful. Blessed are you to Think upon, commune, and *be prayerful* without ceasing; praying so often and continually that your life is a prayer. Prayer is very powerful, since all prayers are heard and answered; and every thought is a prayer, because God hears all thoughts, so *be prayerful*. The way of true prayer is to lay your requests down before the Father, where they become your gifts to Him. Thus you demonstrate that God is all you desire and His love is enough. God knows what you desire and how to bless you, and He will. Your answers always come through guidance and inspiration, so tell your Father that you desire nothing more than Him and no love but His.[34] Lastly, a very good prayer is, 'Thank you, God." So may you pray and *be gratitude now*.

80. Be Abiding. Blessed are you to *be abiding* with me, by believing in me, spending time with me, being attuned and connected to me, and always listening for my voice and guidance. Thus, you will be close to me, *be faith, be trust, be loved by me*, be cared for by me, and be in a close relationship with me, knowing your Self to be my Self as the Christ temple. *Be empowered* by your connection with me and overcome the ego, fear, and guilt. Many times you would have broken down and fallen apart, had it not been for my keeping power. Surely, your joy, peace, well-being and deepest work are achieved by abiding with me, beloved.

---

34 A Course in Miracles (Foundation For Inner Peace, 1975, 1985, 1992), S-1.I.4:4

81. Be Simple. Blessed are you to *be simple* and kind, by *being love* and *being forgiveness*. Simplicity is uncomplicated and as effortless as a positive thought and a gentle word. The ego is complicated since it is insane; Christ is sane and simple as love is, so *be simple*. More so, may you practice the simplicity of peace through forgiveness, which is a clarifying balm soothing ruffled tensions and healing all wounds. *Being peace* and *being simple* as I Am, you will also realize the life, love, and beauty of all creation that transcends the world's polarity. Further, may you see with my eyes in holy vision, acknowledging the magnificence of a simple breath, sunset, and kiss. Verily, Truth is simple and profound, like The New Beatitudes, so *be simple* and *be Truth*. May you especially *be simple* and fulfill God's plan by *being love, being light,* and *being the One Mind* by blessing and healing all Minds as your Self. Then the Holy Spirit and I will provide all your needs and desires, so you might easily and simply dwell upon the rock. Lastly, be sincere and see with my eyes, *being remembrance* that an easy disposition is your own gift. Beloved, *be simple, be Truth,* and *be One* by being the love that you are now.

Chapter 10

Why Achieve Closeness to Me

Now, you might ask, "Why should I achieve closeness to you, Jesus?" And I will answer, saying that you benefit immensely by being close to me because there is no relationship of greater importance.

Verily, every common man and woman is God's One Son, because God has only One Son. Since the Father created you as His beloved Child and I Am God personified, being close to me furthers your closeness to God, since we are One. Furthermore, all of His Children are His Sons and Daughters, being the Christ Self. This is your One Self that is God's Self, the Holy Spirit, and my Self. The innocence and love of God's Self is also within every living being. This is the Truth of being that you are as I Am, and so may you *be*.

Being aligned as One Self, *being the One Mind*, and *being I Am* that, I Am as One, we are unified in purpose to be The New Beatitudes our Selves, which additionally brings us closer together. May you specifically fulfill God's plan and your purpose by *being love, being the light,* and *being the One Mind*. Likewise, in *being One* you will bless and heal all Minds as your Self. Furthermore, *being God's Will, being God's glory,* and *being holy* we are unified in purpose to bless and heal all creation as One. So *be* it!

Being your Self as my Self and One, you may realize me to be your closest friend, ally, and confidant. Lo, I am always with you, I have grand plans for you, and I share your greatest desires in all ways, always. I already know everything about you, all your desires, hopes, and dreams, so I may easily guide you in the way to go and *be*.

I also know your every thought from lifetime to lifetime, all your secret, hidden ideas and desires, and I love you just the same and even more, since I understand you and have compassion for you.

You might note that there are no secrets, nothing is hidden, and everything is known by all who have passed from the earthly dimension. Fortunately, the world is an illusion and all is forgiven. Surely, the Father and I see all as originally created, so *be holy, be innocent,* and *be gratitude now*.

Albeit, there is even more good news! Being close to me and *being trust* in me deepens your dependence upon me and increases the victory in your life. My Will is greater than you might imagine, and anything on earth, and thus I envision grander dreams and infinite expectations for you beyond the physical realm.

Why Achieve Closeness to Me

Especially, fulfilling God's plan and *being God's Will* your Self allows you to live in ease and joy, while depending on God, the Holy Spirit, and me to provide and arrange everything for you. Your intention to bless and heal all life through your holiness is the way that we will heal and bless the world and all creation, and in this intention we are One.

So, fix your eyes upon me and allow your strength to be my strength, and your weakness to be my power. My confidence and surety is yours, and my peace transcends all storms. Surely, my Will is key to being beyond the world in magnitude and empowerment, so *be confident, be empowered*, and *be peace* in all ways, always.

I have said, knock and the door is opened, seek and you shall find, ask and it is given. These are my clear instructions and promises that lead you in the way to overcome illusion and negativity. So, be close to me and witness the pieces of your life falling into perfect place. *Be the One Mind* with me and be sure that my hand is upon you from moment to moment and glory to glory. And lo, watch and see what the Lord will do!

You will find me in the tiniest details and your grandest accomplishments, *being faith* that I am with you all the way. My plans to advance you are beyond time and space, causing the fearful to flee, the earth to give way, and the mountains to fall into the sea.

Being united together in our hearts and One Mind, all things are possible and available now in this present moment. Your awakening, attunement, and alignment are ripe with joyous opportunities to *be*, and your cup is full to overflowing. In the simplicity of love and humility of forgiveness, your grandest creations appear, exist, and manifest as I Am.

Being One, we create together your most magnificent reality now. *Being surrender, being service*, and *being abiding*, love reigns and peace transcends illusion, salvation restores light unto the darkness, and truth inspires you to *be the Christ* temple with your name.

Being close to me, you realize all to *be innocent* as forgiveness restores the memory of holiness and equality. In safety, love extends and expands unto others as It Self. In giving love and *being love*, love is received and returned unto you, being your gift unto your Self. This is the universal circle of life and the love that you are, I Am, and God is.

Within this heavenly realm, miracles appear as numerous as raindrops, being returned unto the giver as God's gentle, compassionate arms encircle and envelop all living souls joyously and eternally as One.

Beholding love as cause and breath of life, God's grace fulfills every desire and need. *Being remembrance* of the Father and effects of His Will, we mirror His glory unto all souls in holy vision. And thus we intend, choose, and *be salvation* for all as One.

In unity, the world is redeemed from the separation that never occurred and illusion is real no more. Only love and God's creations are real, as you behold all with my eyes in holy vision, *being One Mind* and One being.

Being love personified, we live to serve and *be the light* that shines unto the One Mind and heart of God. His Creations express, extend, and remain One, *being the miracle* and being all that is.

Leading the way for those who seek to understand and *be*, salvation is known, revealed, and demonstrated by you, for you, in you, through you, with you and as you, and you within me, *being I Am*. Lo, I Am with you always, being as close as your breath, as loving as your heart, and as certain as life and eternity It Self.

Beloved is your name and love is who you are. Love is your identity, and *being love* is your purpose as I Am and God is. And so will it always *be*, as you come unto me and honor the Father and His example of character, innocence, Oneness, kindness, love, and compassion.

So come unto me and see all your desires amply supplied. Feel the newness of clarity and rise unto your true calling, *being well-being, being blessed,* and *being restored.* Verily, you will never again experience uncertainty or doubt, because Truth reveals the answer to every question in the safety of eternity.

Herein is your grandest truth, deepest love, greatest power and holiest moment, as the common man desires to be the common cause and *be God's Will now.*

To be sure, being close to me you will be these New Beatitudes, which are characteristics of my character and aspects of love, *being I Am* that, I Am now. Beloved, so *be* it.

82. Be Well-Being. Blessed are you to *be well-being* as overall Truth, joy, surrender, alignment, health, ease and abundance. Joy cannot be anything but well-being, since it is God's Will and God's glory for all as One. Thus, you will see everything as a gift, and even thrive in dire circumstances, because the external does not alter your internal, authentic well-being. Being Spirit you will not be insecure; rather you will easily shift from indecision to certainty, *being confident.* So, *be well-being, be abundant* life, value yourself, be positive, be optimistic, *be free* to *be*, and actualize the fullness of your higher Self. The stronger your relationship with me and the more loving and forgiving you are, the more joy and well-being you will *be*.

83. Be Blessed. Blessed are you to *be blessed* and *be loved by God* as Him Self. Blessings are love in action, higher vibrational energy, and gifts from God's heart unto His beloved. *Being an extension of God,* you are blessed to *be One* and *be I Am* that, I Am. You are blessed to be spoken over by the Father and cherished as the beloved. You are also blessed to *be service* and *be sharing* by being a great giver, and to receive the kindness that you give. *Being love,* you will *be a blessing* unto others with your gentle thoughts, words, and actions. You may especially bless all from your open heart and aligned Mind with intentional Thoughts to serve, sustain, restore, and heal. Being obedient when prompted by God, you will *be blessed* as you follow through with His request, no matter how unusual as well. Verily, it is good to *be gratitude* and bless what you already have; then witness its expansion and increase with your intentional Thoughts, choices, and blessings. Lastly, may you speak blessings over your children, praising and reinforcing their good traits and behavior often, being a positive teacher and example of goodness your Self as I Am. For surely, your cup runneth over.

84. Be Endurance. Blessed are you to *be endurance* and overcome the ego by continually asking the Holy Spirit to direct your mind. In so being, you will *be vigilant* in healing your mind and correcting your thinking. Furthermore, when the winds of adversity blow against you, stand tall and do not be moved, *being faith* unto the very end. If a situation is difficult, *be endurance* because there are no challenges for God's One Son. Verily, it is true that hardships produce perseverance, character, and hope. Difficult relationships and circumstances may be released as you ask to *be directed by the Holy Spirit* in being the holy instant, or *being love* rather than fear, judgement, or unforgiveness.

In the moment you desire to *be willing, be surrender,* and request the Holy Spirit to intervene, he will shift the perspectives involved through creative, loving possibilities of release that transform animosity into love. *Being love* you'll see a way in holy vision to *be forgiveness* and release all from judgment and grievances. And in this, beloved, you will *be empowered* and *be endurance.* So *be joy* through trials and feel my presence empowering you to a greater sense of awareness and being. Surely, it has been said that the man in the arena challenging loss of life, limb, and livelihood is the one who rises greatly. On the other hand, comfort and ease produce entitlement, enablement, and lack of character, and this is not the Christ embodiment. Instead, be a visionary, be steadfast, and *be Truth,* enduring the fires of alchemy to *be transformed* from base metal into gold, so to say, or from weakness into strength, from judgment into acceptance, and from bitterness into love. Like the phoenix, Truth gives you dominion over illusion and the power to rise, fly, and *be,* so *be* it!

85. Be Enthusiasm. Blessed are you to *be enthusiasm* in being your divine Self now. I Am is who and what you are, so you will naturally *be enthusiasm.* Joy is God's state of being, and so must you *be* as His extension. *Being enthusiasm* furthers your willingness to be in the flow of life, since there is no uncertainty in I Am. The positive flow of *being surrender, being allowing,* and *being aligned* accelerates passion and enthusiasm, and so may you *be.* All the more, *being the light, being acceptance,* and being optimistic creates positive results, by knowing that there is enough provision of good things for all. May you also enjoy people, gatherings, and community with enthusiasm and passion. Finally, being close to me in a loving relationship, you may *be trust, be confident, be joy, be well-being,* and *be enthusiasm now.*

86. Be Safe. Blessed are you to *be safe* and secure, because no one outside of you can change your Truth or harm your eternal Spirit. So, be with me, *be safe*, and be kept, realizing that your true protection and peace of mind is through God's love. May you will also *be remembrance* that greater is the One who created you, than the things of the world. Even more, as you ask to *be directed by the Holy Spirit* in being more love and forgiveness, you will release your fears and embrace the safety and security of *being the Christ* temple. Finally, *be safe, be guided*, and be wrapped in the robe of the Christ light, which is God's light, love, and power, because I always have your back and all is well.

87. Be Restored. Blessed are you to *be restored* by being these New Beatitudes now. Your innocence has set you free to *be* your greatest Self and create your best life now. So change your mind and *be holy, be whole*, and *be restored* to Oneness. May you also *be directed by the Holy Spirit* in *being forgiveness* so your joy and peace will *be restored*. More so, be amazed that your Father yearns to be in a close relationship with you, as I do, and support you in creating your greatest life now. *Be restored* and awed by my passion for my brothers and sisters, and the power of the Christ Self that we are as I Am. Certainly, God's magnificent Truth has destined mankind to *be restored* and *be the miracle* of love and forgiveness now.

88. Be Sustained. Blessed are you to *be sustained* by God's Truth and love. Acknowledge the Christ as your Self and be sure that God withholds nothing from you. *Be I Am* and be supported, supplied, and sustained as an extension of the Father. No matter what happens in the world, your eternal being will always *be sustained*. Desiring to feel supported and sustained, you may *be confident* in the Oneness of I Am. You may also be comforted by your divine Truth, and secure in the kingdom and glory of all that is. *Being sustained* by God's Will, you will shine and *be the light* unto all who know it not. Furthermore, *being acceptance* of God's holy plan, you are sustained by the Holy Spirit and me in every way, need, and desire as your Self. Finally, may you *be respectful of all life* by assisting every living creature in *being sustained, being safe, being well-being,* and *being loved now.*

89. Be a Channel. Blessed are you to *be a channel* for all to see me through you. The light is my Spirit and strength within you, so *be the light, be strength,* be a messenger, and *be a channel* of divine innocence, love, and power. Even more, be in the flow and be an open channel to give and receive divine love, blessing all with your gentle, beautiful presence. Furthermore, *being an extension of God, being I Am,* and *being a channel* of love and light you acknowledge whose you are, what you are, and why you are here now. Thus, you are love, your purpose is to *be love,* and you are here to fulfill your function and God's plan to be your divine Self. And now God is Self-evident, accessible, and obtainable through you! Ultimately, you will *be the Christ* and *be a channel* of Truth, love, holiness, light, peace, joy and Oneness that heals and uplifts everyone! Finally, may you *be vigilant, be present,* and monitor every thought, word, action, and feeling, being purposeful to *be a channel* of unconditional love as I Am.

Chapter 11

What Happens If You Achieve Closeness to Me

Beloved One, if you achieve closeness to me you will live an uncommon, exceptional, enlightened life. *Being One* who realizes your Self to be the Father's Self, the Holy Spirit, and my Self, you will *be now*. And thus you will be close to God by being the One Son and Christ Child that you are born to *be*.

This is a great place to be, basking in the wonder of our close relationship and friendship. For not only am I your friend, but you are my friend. Being the One Son or Daughter, you and I share a common goal: we mutually love, respect, and honor one another as God's beloved

Child and creation. As I care for you and your concerns, you return the favor and care for mine. You also tend to your purpose and function by fulfilling God's plan. Thus we are One in the awareness, accessibility, and Self-evidence of God's presence through you as your divine Self, so be divine.

How sweet it is to know that we depend on each other, and that I can depend on you to do things for me, to be my friend and give me friendship, service, love, and understanding. How sweet it is, as Jackie Gleason always said, and how dear you are to walk in my sandals with me!

Being close to me you will become like me, for love has called unto your inner being and answered it Self. *Being extensions of God* as I Am, we emulate the character of our Father who has given us life. Being Spirit and being Spiritual you accept, abide, allow, and align your Self with the Father and me by being in a close relationship with us.

Thus, you will also *be love for God* and honor the holiness of your relationship with Him that has been eternally established in Heaven. And herein, you will reach toward the goal which is God.

Being close to me you will *be aligned* with the Holy Spirit and me in love's extension and inclusion, where all life is sacred, holy, and innocent, *being One* breath, One Mind, and One heartbeat.

Being close to me you will acknowledge the vast, eternal Spirit within all, rather than to see only the temporary, physical body. *Being God's Child*, everyone is an extension of the Father's divinity, character, and glory. In this holy instant of awakening, the bright light of Truth shines brilliantly upon the beloved, whose task is not to belittle the personal self but to merge and reconcile it with the magnanimous divine Self that is I Am that, I Am. This is your holy mission to *be* and fulfill now, beloved.

And thus you will be like me and resemble my presence, nature, behavior, virtue, principles, power, and strengths that are exemplified through The New Beatitudes. Many will see God in you and His image reflected in your life, by the all-encompassing love and light that you are. So you will be like God and *be the Christ* with your name by believing, behaving, becoming, and *being love now.*

Being close to me you will acknowledge that love is your power and joy is your strength. The opening of your heart to be more love and be more joy will allow you to experience the wholeness and power of I Am. So you will *be the One Mind* that you are, and only use your Mind to bless and heal others, which is *being acceptance* of God's plan and your function. It is also living a life well lived, beloved.

Your continuous focus upon *being love* and *being joy*, no matter what is going on around you, will deem you a master. Only true masters are undeterred by the drama of the world; instead of participating in egotistical theatrics, they intentionally think and choose to disengage, respond and not react, *be still* and be quiet, while finally tuning and focusing themselves inwardly to the love, joy, peace, and alignment of I Am. Herein they inspire, uplift, and enlighten many to be close to me, *be loved by me*, and *be the Christ* temple with their name. Thus, they are responsible for vast healings and blessings as well, as you may *be* while being The New Beatitudes your Self, beloved.

Practicing closeness to me, you will also *be directed by the Holy Spirit* in *being unconditional forgiveness* automatically. As you continually *be practice* in being the Unconditional Forgiveness Thought you will avoid the reincarnation cycle that sends you back to Earth time and time again until you forgive everyone and everything in all your lifetimes. In this way you will also *be practice* to be the holy instant often, which is *being I Am* that, I Am, while *being trust* in the Holy Spirit to work divinely through you as your Self.

Thus you can see that examining your character is a must, since I have said an unexamined life is not worth living. So, look closely at yourself and see how you may grow, mature, and improve your behavior by being the observer. You are responsible for what you see, while being remembrance of your true identity and purpose. Examine where you may transform your beliefs to better suit your expanding awareness and consciousness, and take corrective measures to be more loving and forgiving.

Likewise, at the end of the day you will *be surrender* of all of your decisions to the Holy Spirit and me. You will monitor your stillness, connection, peace, and intention to *be love, be confident, be guided,* and *be directed* to be your holiest Self now. You will also *be remembrance* of my birth and intention that the world needs "stable" inspiration and influence, and so may you *be*, beloved.

Being close to me, it is a priority for you to *be respectful of all life*. Herein, you will realize the Innocents, who are babies, animals, and nature to be the energy of the Father. Having no ego, they are teachers of unconditional love and forgiveness, so their lives must be honored.[35] *Being One* you will *be remembrance* that what you do unto the Innocents you do unto the Father and your Self.

Further, the Innocents desire to raise the vibration of mankind to heal the Earth. So *be responsible* for all souls

---

35 Sharon Pieroni Day, The Book, The Creator's Template for Eternal Life, (Create Space, Charleston, SC, 2010) p. 93

and all life by *being service* and *being sacrifice* of your personal agenda to assist the Innocents now.

You will also answer the urgent, crucial call to save the rain forest, whose extinction threatens all life. Without air the planet dies, so donate, plant more trees, and be the difference now!

Being close to me you will be these New Beatitude "I Am" Statements of Being as well. By acknowledging, accepting, and visualizing them in your One Mind, you will *be I Am* that, I Am now.

Finally, *being empowered* by these keys to spirituality, you will be radical and *be courageous* in your Truth. You will walk on the water with me, being dominion over all physicality and *being the light* of the world. You will walk with the Father in perfect holiness as well, *being sustained* by the power of God's love. And thus you will be like me, *being the Christ* temple victoriously.

Only love and joy remain, since you desire peace instead of pain and separation, authentic power rather than external power, and Heaven on Earth rather than applause and accolades. So pray only that God's Will be done, because no external thing can equal the Father's desires for His beloved.

Now you might ask, what happens if you don't achieve closeness to me?

Beloved, if you don't achieve closeness to me, you will continue to live in the world, being of the world. You will believe in the illusions of the ego, remaining limited by your beliefs in sin, fear, judgment, and death, rather than fulfilling your divine destiny to *be the Christ* temple.

Even if you are very wealthy and successful in the world, there will always be a hunger and longing for your

Father that cannot be filled by external things. However, you must allow and embrace your internal connection and beingness with I Am, as I Am, to finally be fulfilled.

When you are ready to see things differently, I will take your hand and show you the way. Until then, *be remembrance* that there is a higher power who loves you and desires your love, and He is watching over you now.

Verily as you achieve closeness to me, you will walk on the water by being these New Beatitudes now. So *be* it.

90. *Be Empowered.* Blessed are you to *be empowered* by the love that you are. God is love and so are you, so *be love* and *be empowered*. Truly, your power is inherent within your Self, so it is eternal. On the other hand, the ego says your power is external and within other people and things, being temporary. But you are blessed to be an extension of the powerful One Mind of God that created all things. Aligning your soul or Self with your personality or self is *being authentic power*, which is true power. Authentic power is intrinsic within your divine Self, being permanent, intentional, and authoritative. In contrast, external power is of the world and inherent in things that are temporary, unreal, illusionary, and many times bought with currency. So do not allow things to define you, because things are not who you are. Things can also disappear, and then what happens to your power? It disappears also. Surely, unconditional love is who you are and your power to *be*; so uplift and impact others with your light, non-judgment, and simplicity. Your power is your choice and ability to *be responsible* for the effect or outcome of your cause, which is love. Further, *be intentional choice* to *be empowered* and be great self-esteem, being clarity and *being confident* in being your divine destiny now. *Be practice* in monitoring your thoughts and choices so as to *be authentic*, *be surrender, be allowing,* and *be aligned,* and you will thrive. Surely, *being I Am* is greater than anything in the world, so exchange your worldly strength for my mighty strength and *be empowered now.*

91. Be Courage. Blessed are you to *be courage,* be daring, and be brave in being these New Beatitudes now. Stand tall in the midst of adversity and be fearless, knowing there is nothing to fear because fear is not real. Only love is real and you are love. Follow your heart and do what you must, *being courage* and being bold, because experience is a great teacher. May you also *be courage* in *being acceptance* of the Holy Spirit to be your inner guide, and *be allowing* of Him to direct you in *being forgiveness* unconditionally. May you ask Him to give you the holy instant as well, so you may *be the One Mind* that you are. Likewise, be encouraged when you are valiant enough to be vulnerable and *be responsible* for your deepest feelings and grandest Truth. Further, be encouraged and take risks even if you are timid and unsure, and turn trials into triumphs. In life you will experience setbacks but they give you breathing room and space for rejuvenation and restoration. Continue to *be faith* and be encouraged by my strength, as you watch and see what the Lord will do through you. Take heart from my example and be a hero who saves and serves. You are stronger and more courageous than you can imagine, *being guided* and encouraged by the power that creates worlds. Albeit, you may be weary and battered in physical appearance, but your inherent divine Self is the essential power of life that rises above all external conditions to champion the cause of love that births breath, creates lifeforms, seeds the lands, waters the deserts, fills the oceans, and scatters stars unto the heavens, so *be courage now.*

92. Be Victory. Blessed are you to claim your victory even before your first step, by being close to me. I have an answer for every problem even before you ask, and I have already prepared the way. Surely, you can do all things victoriously, *being the Christ* temple that you are. It is true that when you desire to do great things, resistance will flare up. Yet the authentic power of your love, courage, and faith overturn negativity every time. So continue to overcome doubt by *being courage, being endurance,* being a champion, and *being intentional creation;* in so being you will prophesize your reality and *be victory now.* Lastly, be triumphant and achieve the success of your wildest dreams, *being victorious* love as I Am.

93. Be a Teacher. Blessed are you to *be a teacher* who demonstrates and learns by example. Thus you will *be a teacher* of love and forgiveness, being a role model of awareness in every thought, word, action, and feeling. This is God's plan, that you may *be the light* unto all who are your holy Self as I Am. So shine your love light for all to see, because God is glorified when others see Him in you. Be a leader and an example of righteousness, because God is mighty and so are you. *Be forgiveness* and inspire others to forgive and *be free* from judgment, guilt, and shame. Further, *be the miracle* worker and *be the light* who inspires others to be radical in being your Self. Finally, *be remembrance* that no one can harm your eternal Spirit, because it does not take offense and it cannot be hurt or offended, *being I Am.*

94. Be Allowing. Blessed are you to *be allowing* of your will *to be God's Will,* which is the common cause for the common man. May you also *be allowing* of your connection to God, your true Self, and the Oneness that you are. This is *being salvation* and the greatest thing you can *be.* Allowing is being in constant alignment with Spirit or the

I Am presence within you as well. Even more, *being still* and *being allowing* of my constant communication with you in a livestream, so to say, is the way to *be guided* to your highest good easily. So, allow me to love you and share my being with you by aligning with I Am that I Am. May you additionally allow your mind to *be directed by the Holy Spirit* and *be forgiveness* automatically. More so, be close to me and *be allowing* of my strength and power to be yours, by asking and receiving. May you also release your resistance and be relieved that all is well, because it is. Albeit, do not resist your inherent joy, wholeness, and worthiness: rather, *be allowing* of your connection to God and let your Self *be*. Lastly, rest and allow yourself to relax and meditate, *be still, be surrender*, be in the flow, *be joy, be love, be gratitude*, and *be I Am* that, I Am.

95. Be Strength. Blessed are you to *be strength* and the power of Christ as your divine Self. *Being God's Will* as your will, you will *be strength*. True strength is not found in the world, but within your Self as the love that you are. You will increase your strength by being more love and more joy. Surely, you can do all things through Christ who strengthens you. So lead with strength and conquer the impossible with unwavering integrity and perseverance. More so, be sure that your troubles do not impede your progress but increase your problem solving abilities. Because a problem is for you, being a pro-blem or way for things to change for the better and you to grow stronger. As changes unfold, new powers converge to increase your alignment. You have all the strength you need to overcome, conquer, and *be victorious*, for I Am always triumphant, and so shall you *be!* Beloved, you need nothing outside of your Self, because you are authentically, intrinsically, and innatcly the strength and power to *be*.

96. Be Enlightened. Blessed are you to *be enlightened* by awakening from the dream of illusion to be your divine Self. As light and understanding shift your perspective, you will see in holy vision. Realizing you are Spirit in a physical body, and an extension of the Father, you will *be Truth* and *be enlightened*. *Being aware* that only love is real, you will not think thoughts of fear, sin, and death anymore, because they are negative and illusionary. What is real is God's Truth, which rests upon the foundation of innocence, love, joy, and peace. Enlightenment is *being God's Will* and *being Truth* as I Am; whereby you intentionally create and align your Self with Source by monitoring your behavior. It is true that *being enlightened* is the highest level of consciousness possible, and it is achieved through *being light, being love, being joy,* and *being peace* as I Am. So, see clearly now, wake up, be self-actualized as I Am, *be the light, be love, be joy, be peace,* and *be enlightened now.* So *be* it!

97. Be Sacrifice. Blessed are you to *be sacrifice* by doing for others before yourself, and respecting and serving the Innocents as the energy of the Father. The Innocents are babies, animals, and nature and they are teachers of unconditional love and forgiveness, so they must be honored. Even more, I greatly appreciate the sacrifice of your personal daily desires to *be the Christ* with your name, as I ask you to tend to another for me by doing what matters most. For, when your cup is full to overflowing you have no ego, needs, or identities; you naturally serve by *being God's Will, being One,* and *being respect for all life.* Finally, serving others through sacrifice is greatly redemptive, being true worship and divine giving[36] as Sharon Day, founder of Healing Hearts Animal Rescue, knows all too

---

36 Sharon Pieroni Day, The Book, The Creator's Template for Eternal Life, (Create Space, Charleston, SC,2010) p. 93

well. Truthfully, you merely sacrifice and give up illusions and false perceptions, while only God's creations remain. Therefore, there is no real sacrifice; yet in the world of duality there will be times that you do for others before yourself, and in the moment it is a sacrifice. Herein, the blessing is to put others first in joy, service, and appreciation by being your Self in the moment, and not yourself. As you do for others before yourself, by expressing and expanding love, you exponentially experience love for all life as your Self and One. Thus, I honor your service and giving, for this is the way to be a temple of love and find your Self. Indeed, the release of false beliefs restores your mind to innocence and love. So release illusion, suffering, sadness, negativity, judgment, guilt, and attack, and *be allowing* of your Self to awaken and *be love, be joy, be peace*, and *be now.*

98. Be Heaven on Earth. Blessed are you to *be Heaven on earth* by *being forgiveness* of everything and everyone, including yourself. Heaven is here now when you unconditionally forgive all, since Heaven is not a place,[37] but the Truth and Oneness of your being. It is also the higher vibrational alignment of I Am with your awareness, so *be allowing, be aligned,* and *be love* as God loves. *Being Heaven on earth* is *being I Am*, by choosing and allowing your Self to *be the miracle.* All the more, in *being forgiveness* God replaces all of your unhappy memories with only happy recollections, and everything old is new again. Albeit, Wayne Dyer said it best when he stated that Heaven on earth is a choice you make, not a place to find. So, fulfill your purpose, *be forgiveness, be the light, be authentic, be intentional creation, be free,* be playful and light hearted and exit the world of judg-

---

37 A Course In Miracles, Inc., (FOUNDATION FOR INNER PEACE, 1975, 1985, 1992), T-18.VI.1:5

ment to dance in the realms of Heaven on earth. Simply stated, Heaven is being Home again by being these New Beatitudes now. So *be* it.

Part Four

GRACE AND GRATITUDE

Chapter 12

Be Grace

God's grace is amazing as the popular hymn so eloquently states. In infinite grace, the Father gives you Him Self and His being as your Self. Thus, you are Spirit, and Spirit is always in a state of grace.

God's grace is the Holy Spirit's power that directs you in the way to *be love*. Grace is a trait of your real Self, and sufficient unto it Self and your Self, so *be God's Child, be authentic,* and *be grace now.*

Grace is given to you freely because you are God's beloved Child and One Son. By the grace of God, you are innocent and free to *be the light* of your Father as One.

In God's Will, grace is acceptance of God's love.[38] *Being grace* and *being love* you will *be restored* to your original state of being as I Am.

Verily, grace is acceptance that never resists the natural flow of life. Grace also sees only the good and magnifies it, *being the way*.

Certainly, there is infinite grace in forgiveness, so *be unconditional forgiveness* of everyone and everything. Miracles occur naturally through grace, when forgiveness is given and everyone is released by the power of love, so *be love now*.

Finally, *being grace*, you will *be sacrifice* for the Innocents, promoting their welfare before yourself. The lessons that the Innocents teach mankind are life changing and lifesaving, so adopt a pet and save a life today. Surely, the life you save is your own, *being One*.

Herein, the following New Beatitudes reflect the grace that you are as the Christ Child. Beloved, so *be* it.

99. Be Grace. Blessed are you to be Spirit, since Spirit is always in a state of grace. So, you can only *be grace* as I Am. Grace is your natural state of complete abundance and the remembrance of One as One. God's grace is given to you because you are His beloved Child and One Son. Many say that grace is unmerited because of supposed sin. Yet *being remembrance* that sin is not real, being a product of the ego and its false beliefs, we see that the Father has not forgiven sin because all are innocent and there is nothing to forgive. Albeit, you all are playing the game of life in the illusion, whereby you correctly remember that only love and its creations are real. Thus, innocence is the Father's energy and presence, being the true state of

---

[38] A Course in Miracles (Foundation For Inner Peace, 1975, 1985, 1992), W-pI.169.2:1

mind on His Son. So, *be innocent, be grace,* and *be the One Mind* in joy and freedom to *be* and create your life anew. God's grace is amazing and infinite, being your Father's extension of Him Self as your Self. Surely, this spiritual perspective is different from traditional religious beliefs, but I ask you to *be open-minded, be loved by God, be loved by me, be love for yourself, be innocent, be free, be peace, be resurrection, be renunciation, be transformed,* and *be grace* now. So *be* it, beloved.

100. Be Mercy. Blessed are you to *be mercy* as I Am. The Father is merciful and so should you *be* as His extension. In His infinite kindness your Father gives only mercy, compassion, and grace, and so may you *be*. So give as you have received, being so compassionate and understanding consistently that you will *be mercy*. In His infinite mercy God only sees equal extensions of Him Self. It does not matter what you think you have done, because you are innocent; and in so being your Father is truly merciful. *Being trust* in God you will *be mercy* as well. Lastly, *be mercy, be One,* and forget the past; instead see goodness within every face that is mine and yours in holy vision. For the other is your Self, my Self, the Holy Spirit, and God as I Am.

101. Be Patient. Blessed are you to *be patient* and resilient with a lack of complaint. Time is of this world and not Heaven, so *be eternal* and be timeless. *Be patient* and *be trust* in the stillness of the Father. The perfect answer will always *be now* as you continue to focus on God's certainty. *Be faith* and do not be anxious for anything, *being trust* in my divine timing for your highest good. Being sure of love and all possibilities to *be*, you may *be patient* in peace, joy, and well-being. Beloved, all is well and always will *be,* because your Truth is absolute and miracles abound timelessly.

102. Be Honest. Blessed are you to *be honest* and *be aligned* with your greatest Self. In all your thoughts, words and actions may you be sincere and be truthful, being from your heart. Honesty gives you peace of mind, which is a reflection of the Oneness that you are. So *be honest* with yourself, believe the Truth, live the Truth, and *be Truth*. *Be willing* to face your fears honestly and courageously, so they may be forgiven and released. Beloved, walk your talk, be true to your word, be impeccable, and *be honest* in your intentional choice for God.

103. Be Just. Blessed are you to *be non-judgment* and *be just* with all who are God and your Self. Salvation is God's justice and the way you are restored to wholeness.[39] May you also realize everyone to *be innocent* and sinless, *being just*. Forgiveness is the way of *being acceptance, being tolerance,* and *being just* for One and all. Equality brings forth justice and clarity, *being God's Will* and glory for all who are already deserving. The ego has convinced you that you are imperfect and incomplete, so it must be justly overcome.

104. Be Gentle. Blessed are you to *be gentle* and be kind as I Am. Gentleness is love, compassion, goodwill, acceptance, and willingness to yield. Gentleness is the essence of the Father and the core of all beings. Love is gentle and kind, yet stronger than any Earthly power. So, be strong yet gentle and try a little tenderness, as the popular song says, because only kindness will help and heal. As it has been said, kindness turns away wrath, when nothing but love will do. And if you make a mistake don't beat yourself up, since true generosity is of the Spirit. So *be gentle* toward all who seek to *be loved* and *be accepted*, because that is what everyone desires.

---

[39] A Course in Miracles (Foundation For Inner Peace, 1975, 1985, 1992), M-19.4:1&2

105. Be Self-Control. Blessed are you to *be self-control,* be stable, *be the light,* and be calm by dwelling upon me and allowing your light to shine. Your emotions are evidence and insight into how you really feel, so trust them and the guidance they provide. If you feel good, you are allowing love and *being aligned* with your inner being. If you don't feel well, you are not allowing love, so you are not aligned with your Self or me. So *be aware* when negativity arises, and do not react hastily. Instead, be unmoved, be calm, be restraint, and respond with forethought and forgiveness, *being a channel* of my Spirit and power. *Be intentional breath, be intentional Thought,* and *be intentional choice* to *be self-control* and you will *be abiding, be blessed,* and *be empowered.* Stability comes from *being trust* in God and your Self, so *be self-control* and *be still.* Finally, *be remembrance* of my example of self-control that you may *be now* as I Am.

106. Be Still. Blessed are you to *be still* and know that I Am God. *Be still* and listen to the quiet, small voice within that is your Self, God's Self, the Holy Spirit, and my Self. *Be still* and be dedicated to be from your heart, *being One* with all living beings. *Be intentional breath* in the holiness of this now moment, *being aware* of each inhale and exhale. *Be still,* be rest, and practice meditation for at least five minutes a day, being in a high conscious connection with God. May you also *be still* and practice a morning meditation to set your day aright. *Be still* and *be aware* of the silence between the thoughts as well, being attuned to the presence of I Am that I Am. Beloved, you may *be peace* and *be still* through Christ who rests you.

Chapter 13

Be Gratitude

True gratitude is a deep appreciation of the divinity and presence of your higher Self, being life, *being Truth,* and *be*-ing. Gratitude is powerful beyond the temporary things of the world, because it is unaffected by false beliefs. Herein, *being gratitude* is *being joy* in the Truth of your divine Self and this holy, empowerment teaching.

Acknowledging the energy of gratitude will align you in the way of living and *be*-ing The New Beatitudes. The power of appreciation is inviting, being joyously perceptible, uplifting and inspiring. *Being practice* to *be grateful* for everything right where you are now, is the way to become gratitude and *be gratitude.* Thus your limiting beliefs dissolve, old habits are released, life is anew, and synchronicity unfolds. You now see life with fresh eyes in holy vision, *being free* to *be!*

It is good to *be gratitude* for everything, no matter how things appear. Continuing to be thankful with intention, your mind will release its negative tendency and adapt to your positive momentum. Life will then only deliver good things because you deliberately choose only the good by *being free* will. Designing your reality intentionally is a quantum physics theory. Your thoughts and expectations are the way you create your reality, so expect only good and things will get better. Even more, *being love* continually will give you more to *be gratitude* for, so *be love* and observe everyone and everything being more loving.

You will truly *be aligned* with the Oneness of your Self as you appreciate the Oneness of another. And *being God's Child*, you will *be gratitude* that your identity is Spirit and love, and your purpose is to *be love,* since love is the way to *be.*

You may also *be gratitude* that your purpose is also to *be forgiveness* automatically, so you will be non-judgment, blameless, and guiltless, and so will everyone else. And thus, you will truly *be unconditional forgiveness* and heal yourself.

Verily, you may *be gratitude* that all is well in God's Will and God's glory. All of God's goodness and abundance is already yours, so *be already deserving, be blessed, be well-being,* and praise God now.

It is also good to be appreciation as naturally as breathing, and take nothing for granted in continual thankfulness for the awesome ordinary. Say "thank you" often and be grateful for every sunrise, this beautiful planet to dance upon, and the intelligence of your being. See with my eyes in holy vision and behold the wonder of all life, being grateful for the sacredness of this now moment to express, experience, elevate, lighten up, smile, laugh, share, shine, go with the flow, *be joy,* be adventure, and be fun.

In so being, you may *be discipline, be vigilant,* and *be intentional choice* to focus on everything that is good, holy, and orderly. Furthermore, be grateful and allow my light to naturally fill and transform every cell. *Being aligned* with my presence, you will *be practice, be gratitude, be joy* and *be well-being* as I Am.

As you know, many people are characterized by their positive attitude of gratitude. Surely, *being gratitude* is the way to flourish and *be.* As you desire to *be gratitude,* you will focus on your good and vibrate at a higher frequency, magnetizing more good to you by the powerful law of attraction. May you will *be gratitude* for your body as well, and the temple of God that it provides your Spirit as a presence of love and light in the world.

May you also *be gratitude* for the Innocents, who are dependent upon your awareness of their mission to heal mankind. To be sure, your relationship with the Innocents directly reflects your soul's relationship with the Father. Certainly, as awareness increases the Innocents will be honored and euthanasia will not be an option at animal shelters. [40]

Expanding upon *being love* and *being gratitude* for what is, and all that you are, you will be your divine destiny and ascend above the earthly plane. As I have said, this is your soul's purpose and the way to *be.* In every loving thought, word, action, and feeling you ascend and rise above negativity and fear to express, experience, and explore your glorious nature and character that is an extension of the

---

[40] Sharon Pieroni Day, The Book, The Creator's Template for Eternal Life, (Create Space, Charleston, SC, 2010) p 109 & 113

Spirituality For The Common Man

Father. So *be gratitude, be now,* and dwell within the higher realms of Heaven when you return Home.

Indeed, balancing more than one half or fifty-one percent of your karma is fulfilling your divine mission to *be the Christ* temple and the way to avoid reincarnation again in another physical body on earth. *Being love* and *being forgiveness* unconditionally clears your karma and allows your ascension now. More so, *being intentional choice* to *be One* with all life is *being enlightened, being ascension,* and being these New Beatitudes as I Am.

And thus you will fulfill God's plan by *being mindful* to *be love, be the light, be a blessing,* and heal all. In so doing the Holy Spirit and I will fulfill your every need and desire, while arranging everything for your highest good. This is our promise to you while vigilance, discipline, and simplicity guide your creations. Being steadfast in this cause deems you to *be the miracle* worker, *be a healer,* and *be the light* worker, and so may you *be.*

Herein, these New Beatitudes are the way to *be gratitude* and *be the Christ* temple of your life now. Beloved, so *be* it.

107. Be Gratitude. Blessed are you to *be gratitude* for everything. Practicing an attitude of gratitude multiplies your good and brings more good to you. Being grateful also releases the abundance of life, making what is enough. So, be thankful and see the glass as half full, rather than half empty. I Am is enough, being much more than the world can imagine; it is you greatest calling and most fulfilling, divine destiny. Finally, be grateful for everything, since you receive gifts and opportunities from your difficulties that otherwise would not be.

108. Be Generous. Blessed are you to give generously to your brothers and sisters, because what you do for them you do for God and your Self. For it is through your brother and sister that you receive what you give, so *be generous*. May you also be a great giver and give freely to those less fortunate than you, *being abundant*. May you also *be generous* with your time, light, joy, and compassion, realizing that inspiration is as easy as a gentle touch, kind word, or simple act of faith. Likewise, *being generous* to do and *be* for others before your Self and as your Self multiplies the energy and blesses all exponentially. Finally, *be remembrance* that you receive what you give, because all is One, so *be generous*.

109. Be Open-Minded. Blessed are you to see things differently by *being open-minded*. See the reality of love and behold the Christ that is One with you, and actually your Self, rather than the perceptions and limitations of the world. *Be open-minded* by denying guilt and judgment, since the happenings you imagine are mere projections of your thoughts. *Be non-judgment* and do not see the speck in another's eye, because there isn't one. Only see with my eyes, being holy vision for all your brothers and sisters as One. *Be open-minded* and *be allowing* of your limitless good, *being God's Child*. More so, *be resurrection*, be redemption, and *be the light* that you are as Spirit, rather than anything less than your miraculous, perfect Self. Surely, love is the key to *being open-minded*, seeing all creation as beautiful and good as I Am.

110. Be a Friend. Blessed are you to *be a friend* and *be One*. Friendship is the proving ground of brotherly love, forgiveness, acceptance, and non-judgment. Surely, I am your closest friend, for you are within me as my Self. No one knows you better or loves you more, since your every thought and breath are mine. Being the salt of the earth, you will *be understanding* and *be compassion* for others, inspiring them to be their divine Self by your extraordinary example. Even more, salt improves flavor and so may you *be*, as you inspire more love and joy in a dualistic world of fear and negativity. Beloved, be my friend and befriend yourself by *being the Golden Rule, being honest,* being loyal, *being joy,* laughing at yourself, and *being the light* that you are now. Finally, *being One* with all as One, everyone is your friend. So have no enemies, since this would require you to be judgmental and hold grievances, and this need not *be*. Instead, *be remembrance* that there is no separation in the One and *be a friend* now.

111. Be Abundant. Blessed are you to *be abundant* and prosperous in the priceless Truth of your being. Abundance is God in action and life itself, being the fullness and supply of the Father. Abundance and prosperity are yours already, since you are provided for by the very nature of your being. So you are more than abundant; you are abundance! Things that can be bought and taken away are temporary and not true abundance. Albeit, abundance is a product of your innate worthiness, wholeness, integrity, and character, being internal and not external, and in this you are rich. There is a natural abundance for all, because shortage is only a perception of separation, and there is no separation. Furthermore, holding grievances will block your abundance, beloved, so *be love, be non-judgment, be forgiveness,* and *be gratitude.* Herein, celebrate the Christ temple that you are and create more of what is desired by your powerful, intentional thoughts and intentional choices to give freely and *be now*. More so, *be aware* that joy is your success and directly related to the love that you intrinsically are, *being I Am*. Lastly, *be abundant* and give freely to all, trust and tithe, know that prosperity comes from God and you are not alone, and choose to follow me successfully now. *Being God's Will* and being dominion over the world, you will always *be abundant, be blessed*, be prosperous, and *be empowered now.*

112. Be Order. Blessed are you to *be God's Will* and *be order.*[41] God's Will orders your life, replacing the dream of illusion with Truth. God's Will is perfect, joyous, and loving, being all good things for the greatest good of all. Everything happens in divine order and according to God's plan individually and collectively, for a reason and beneficial lesson. The universe is ordered so that you learn precisely what you desire and need right now. When you are not aligned and out of order with God's Will, your life will reflect the imbalance. But alas, the prodigal son is always divinely directed and welcomed home with great celebration! Surely, there are no coincidences because the universe is ordered for you to receive exactly what is relevant to your cause each moment, being the effects of what you give. Even the most painful experiences are essential to your greatest growth and abundance. Albeit, you may be sure that all is in divine order and that all is well. For I Am a God of order, and when the way is unclear I will guide you in the way to remove the blocks to your clarity, joy, success, and divine destiny now. So beloved, *be order now* since this is your time to shine and moment to *be!*

113. Be the Kingdom of God. Blessed are you to be God's Word, law, Will, and Christ temple, *being the Kingdom of God*. The keys to the Kingdom are The New Beatitudes that guide you in the way to *be*, and thus they are *be* attitudes. Verily, the Kingdom of God is within you, being your divine Self, the Christ consciousness, and the fulfillment and presence of God as the Christ Child and Christ temple. So be nurtured by your alignment with me,

---

[41] A Course in Miracles(Foundation For Inner Peace, 1975, 1985, 1992), T-7, IV.2:3&4

because there is no higher calling or realization of your own consciousness than *being God's Will*. Being the Sons and Daughters of the Father, you are Truth, innocence, love, joy, and peace. So may God's Kingdom come and *be now* as I Am.

114. Be Ascension. Blessed are you to *be the One Mind* and be from your heart, which is *being ascension*. Surely, *being love* and *being forgiveness* is *being ascension* beyond the worldly plane. Verily, I am speaking of energetic ascension, or Christ consciousness transcendence, which is not physical but spiritual. Rising above the limitations of the world and the ego to *be Heaven on Earth*, is your greatest potential, true purpose and divine destiny now. So see with my eyes in holy vision and behold the Christ Self that you are by *being ascension* and being these New Beatitudes now.

This higher consciousness is the alignment of the Photon Belt and your shift within it to *be unconditional love* your Self. The plan for this ascension began fifty thousand years ago and culminated with the 2012 energy shift and the Dispensation of Love.

Furthermore, *being love* you will also *be compassion* by *being mercy* and *being passion* for your brothers and sisters, *being One* as One. This is the leading edge of awareness, evolution, and being that mankind will shift to and *be aligned* with. It is also ascension from the darkness and victimhood of the third dimension, into the awareness of the fourth dimension, and the beingness of the fifth dimension respectively, which The New Beatitudes call you to *be now*.

There will finally *be peace* on Earth when individuals *be love, be One, be compassion*, and *be respect for all life* innately them Selves. Inner peace cannot be contained, because it is like love, gently filling, soothing, and flowing from One to another and another as One. The power is within each One to *be love*, *be peace*, and *be healed*; so let it begin with you now, beloved. So *be* it!

With that said, are you willing to help me change the world? Are you willing to be the leader and light that shines the way for those who know it not? For salvation lives within another who is you, and the Oneness that is your collective, infinite Self. As you do for others as God indwelling, you will be the change that saves the world and shifts the collective consciousness to love, joy, and enlightenment. It is time to be the living personification of The New Beatitudes and change the world for the better. Now is the time to rise, shine, and *be!*

Beloved, these are The New Beatitudes that I give you now. These keys to spirituality will unlock your ability to be Self-realized, as you desire to *be*. They will cause your consciousness and soul to evolve and reside in a higher realm in Heaven for all eternity. They are also a global force for good and humanity's power for real change and ascension as well.

So, rise from the dead or that which no longer serves you, and use the New Beatitudes as tools for living and being that enable you to be in a close relationship with your Father, the Holy Spirit, me, your brothers and sisters, and all living beings. Practice being them, along with seeing in holy vision, reveling in your holy relationships, being the holy instant, and *being intentional choice* to *be directed by the Holy Spirit* and you will realize your Self to be a divine human, or more simply put, be divine!

Having embraced this journey that is all about your soul's evolution, your real identity, your true purpose, the illusion of the world, the innocence of all living beings, your intentional creations, your relationship with God, your relationship with others, and the importance of grace and gratitude, you will be certain that you are within me as all that is.

After all, you have contractually agreed to be here now. You have ventured forth once again unto the darkness, so that you may *be One, be the light,* and be the change that is so deeply desired at this time. *Being One,* you will embrace a global awareness and consciousness of One for All and All as One, and so shall you *be now.*

The evolution of mankind will shift as these empowerments for being are realized, and salvation will come unto everyone by their own love and forgiveness. You will uplift the collective consciousness of the planet as you actualize these New Beatitudes, by *being the Christ* temple with your name.

Now, behold the prodigal Son who has returned unto His Father's embrace, by *being remembrance* of the love that you are. You finally know who you are, what you are, and why you are here now.

The Christ Child is who you are and always will *be,* since your journey into illusion has ceased to exist through the opening of your heart, the healing of your Mind, and the correction of your thoughts. The Christ temple, Mind, and consciousness being reconciled with the human self and personality, with no separation, is what The New Beatitudes inspire you to *be.*

Surely, you will *be now* as you walk with me hand in hand unto the Kingdom of God that you are as I Am. The search for meaning has ended, the answers have been revealed, and the Truth has set you free to *be* divinely human and be divine now!

All your fears have vanished into the nothingness that they were, and your mind has been restored unto the One Mind that it will always *be.*

Be Gratitude

Peace is your mindset, love is your watchword, and forgiveness is the way unto Heaven and your eternal Home where you reside beside me. The Truth and joy of the Christ Child is Self-evident, as you realize your Self to be the visible likeness of God.

Thus, may the common man be united in a common cause: *be God's Will now.* And so may you *be*, beloved, being returned to the Oneness, innocence, love, and joy that you are, being all that is and *being I Am* that, I Am as God is.

Appendix

The New Beatitudes

1. Be God's Will
2. Be God's Glory
3. Be I Am
4. Be One
5. Be Truth
6. Be God's Child
7. Be Eternal
8. Be Holy
9. Be Remembrance
10. Be Awakened
11. Be an Extension of God
12. Be Now
13. Be Respectful of All Life
14. Be Resurrection
15. Be the Christ

Spirituality For The Common Man

16. Be Authentic
17. Be the Golden Rule
18. Be Salvation
19. Be Renunciation
20. Be the Way
21. Be the Light
22. Be the Atonement
23. Be Love
24. Be Loved by God
25. Be Love for God
26. Be Loved by Me
27. Be Love for Yourself
28. Be Love for One Another
29. Be the One Mind
30. Be the Miracle
31. Be Joy
32. Be Innocent
33. Be Forgiveness
34. Be Directed by the Holy Spirit
35. Be Non-Judgment
36. Be Acceptance
37. Be Compassion
38. Be Tolerance
39. Be Defenseless
40. Be Healed
41. Be Vigilant
42. Be Whole
43. Be Equal
44. Be Free
45. Be Faith
46. Be Detached
47. Be Transformed
48. Be Discipline

The New Beatitudes

49. Be Peace
50. Be Already Deserving
51. Be Guided
52. Be Infinite
53. Be Beauty
54. Be Confident
55. Be Wisdom
56. Be Balance
57. Be Hope
58. Be Responsible
59. Be Aware
60. Be Aligned
61. Be Intentional Creation
62. Be Present
63. Be Intentional Breath
64. Be Intentional Thought
65. Be Intentional Choice
66. Be Practice
67. Be Trust
68. Be Intuition
69. Be Integrity
70. Be Understanding
71. Be Passion
72. Be Imagination
73. Be in the World but not of the World
74. Be Surrender
75. Be Willing
76. Be Humble
77. Be Service
78. Be Sharing
79. Be Prayerful
80. Be Abiding
81. Be Simple

82. Be Well-Being
83. Be Blessed
84. Be Endurance
85. Be Enthusiasm
86. Be Safe
87. Be Restored
88. Be Sustained
89. Be a Channel
90. Be Empowered
91. Be Courage
92. Be Victory
93. Be a Teacher
94. Be Allowing
95. Be Strength
96. Be Enlightened
97. Be Sacrifice
98. Be Heaven on Earth
99. Be Grace
100. Be Mercy
101. Be Patient
102. Be Honest
103. Be Just
104. Be Gentle
105. Be Self-Control
106. Be Still
107. Be Gratitude
108. Be Generous
109. Be Open-Minded
110. Be a Friend
111. Be Abundant
112. Be Order
113. Be the Kingdom of God
114. Be Ascension

The New Beatitudes "I Am" Statements of Being

Beloved, the powerful words you think or speak following "I Am" create your life, so *be intentional creation.* It is good to *be* your divine Self by thinking and speaking positively to command and declare your most magnificent destiny now. You may *be I Am* that, I Am also as you practice and declare the "I Am" Statements of Being herein, and so may you *be.*

1. I Am God's Will
2. I Am God's Glory
3. I Am That I Am
4. I Am One
5. I Am Truth
6. I Am God's Child

Spirituality For The Common Man

7. I Am Eternal
8. I Am Holy
9. I Am Remembrance
10. I Am Awakened
11. I Am an Extension of God
12. I Am Now
13. I Am Respectful of All Life
14. I Am Resurrection
15. I Am the Christ
16. I Am Authentic
17. I Am the Golden Rule
18. I Am Salvation
19. I Am Renunciation
20. I Am the Way
21. I Am the Light
22. I Am the Atonement
23. I Am Love
24. I Am Loved by God
25. I Am Love for God
26. I Am Loved by Jesus
27. I Am Love for Myself
28. I Am Love for One Another
29. I Am the One Mind
30. I Am the Miracle
31. I Am Joy
32. I Am Innocent
33. I Am Forgiveness
34. I Am Directed by the Holy Spirit
35. I Am Non-Judgment
36. I Am Acceptance
37. I Am Compassion
38. I Am Tolerance
39. I Am Defenseless

The New Beatitudes "I Am" Statements of Being

40. I Am Healed
41. I Am Vigilant
42. I Am Whole
43. I Am Equal
44. I Am Free
45. I Am Faith
46. I Am Detached
47. I Am Transformed
48. I Am Discipline
49. I Am Peace
50. I Am Already Deserving
51. I Am Guided
52. I Am Infinite
53. I Am Beauty
54. I Am Confident
55. I Am Wisdom
56. I Am Balance
57. I Am Hope
58. I Am Responsible
59. I Am Aware
60. I Am Aligned
61. I Am Intentional Creation
62. I Am Present
63. I Am Intentional Breath
64. I Am Intentional Thought
65. I Am Intentional Choice
66. I Am Practice
67. I Am Trust
68. I Am Intuition
69. I Am Integrity
70. I Am Understanding
71. I Am Passion
72. I Am Imagination

73. I Am in the World but not of the World
74. I Am Surrender
75. I Am Willing
76. I Am Humble
77. I Am Service
78. I Am Sharing
79. I Am Prayerful
80. I Am Abiding
81. I Am Simple
82. I Am Well-Being
83. I Am Blessed
84. I Am Endurance
85. I Am Enthusiasm
86. I Am Safe
87. I Am Restored
88. I Am Sustained
89. I Am a Channel
90. I Am Empowered
91. I Am Courage
92. I Am Victory
93. I Am a Teacher
94. I Am Allowing
95. I Am Strength
96. I Am Enlightened
97. I Am Sacrifice
98. I Am Heaven on Earth
99. I Am Grace
100. I Am Mercy
101. I Am Patient
102. I Am Honest
103. I Am Just
104. I Am Gentle
105. I Am Self-Control

The New Beatitudes "I Am" Statements of Being

106. I Am Still
107. I Am Gratitude
108. I Am Generous
109. I Am Open-Minded
110. I Am a Friend
111. I Am Abundant
112. I Am Order
113. I Am the Kingdom of God
114. I Am Ascension

A Memoriam to Harvey Carter Lane, Jr.

Be Eternal
Dad's NDE

Since publishing this book in 2011, I witnessed the death of my beloved father, Harvey Carter Lane, Jr. on September 11, 2015.

I have added this memoriam because of the understanding it adds to Jesus's New Beatitude, *be eternal*, and its real life experience of death and life after death.

My Father passed of kidney failure due to cancer and diabetes. He left behind a great legacy of love and forgiveness which we can all aspire to, and he is forever remembered as our beloved "Daddy-Bear."

During Dad's illness he suffered through the complete loss of his mobility, several strokes, renal failure, and a coma. He was finally moved to hospice where he lived for eleven excruciating days. During his 42 hour coma he amazingly experienced a Near Death Experience and lived to tell about it. With difficult and limited speech he spoke of traveling towards the light and arriving in Heaven to see Jesus, "who was a saint." He also saw his mother, father, dear sister Lillian, favorite Uncle Calvin, many angels, and our departed pets. He spoke of seeing my mother, Marion Lane, and "how she loved us all with a never ending love."

I videotaped Dad's NDE narrative as he lay in ICU at Sentara Virginia Beach General Hospital, and his final, short videos are posted on my website, www.spiritualityforthecommonman.com. They are titled *Be Eternal*, Dad's NDE.

This experience was his final gift to me. It is validation of The New Beatitudes from Jesus Christ and my role as his messenger. It is also verification of The New Beatitude *be eternal* and the continuation of life after death.

Dad shifted as he understood the eternal nature of the soul, and accepted his passing as a healing and release from fatal disease. Dad was a changed man after his NDE, being peaceful, calm, and acquiescent. He no longer feared death but understood it as a continued journey for his spirit and soul. He was excited about the great life he had lived, and the work he was to perform in the afterlife, which was ministering to young fathers and inspiring them to deeply love their children. He was happy to be released from his physical body that no longer served him, and now enjoys running along the beaches of the Chesapeake Bay in Spirit form. He also likes moving quickly and flying wherever and to whomever he thinks about easily!

Being employed in his youth with the Navy as an airplane mechanic and later as a supervisory specialist with the Blue Angels, he is literally in seventh heaven! He has visited me several times through divine guidance and is quite a chatterbox. He knows what is going on here on earth and in my life, what is going to happen in the future, and has access to all knowledge, answering any question I ask.

Dad was not a religious man but became interested in spirituality after living with me for almost five years before his passing. After his NDE he said that my awareness of spiritual principles is accurate and he supports my ministry more enthusiastically than ever.

I honor and thank Dad for his final gift and loving intention to share his experience with those who might fear death, because we all eventually pass from this earthly plane. Dad realized that we reunite in Oneness with All; how you label All is an individual preference, but Dad and I address All as God, Jesus, the Holy Spirit, the Blessed Mother, and All Divine Spirit. He said death is nothing to fear but the natural progression of our souls. He also said that Heaven is beautiful beyond belief, the reward for living life, and the gift for fulfilling our sacred contracts.

Dad was solemn yet peaceful about returning to Heaven. He was sad to leave his family, but assured us that we would all be fine and eventually reunite there together. Until then he guaranteed us that he would stay in touch in the numerous ways Spirit communicates within the many dimensions, and he has.

Always *being gratitude* for Dad's love, life, the final gift of his NDE, his peaceful passage to eternity, and continued presence, I profess my devoted love for him and all divine Spirit. I appreciate God and Jesus' support and everlasting love for us all, the joy of life, and the continued life of our soul's expansion into eternity.

Certainly, we will all rest, *be joy, be peace, be eternal,* run, fly, express, and continue to experience life with a new perspective in due time and for all time, until it is our time to pass from this life into the forevermore.

I hope you find comfort in Dad's NDE and the profound Truth of The New Beatitudes, and I thank you for your interest, spiritual advancement, and awareness now. May God bless us all, so *be* it, and Amen.

Always *being love* and *being gratitude,*
Keith Davis

About the Author

Keith Davis' abiding love of Jesus led her on this fantastic spiritual journey. She is grateful to be the messenger for this teaching, and the opportunity to fulfill her divine mission successfully. She has walked through the fire in her life and exited the flames being more loving, compassionate, resilient, and kind because of her deep faith in God and close relationship with Jesus and the Holy Spirit.

She resides in Virginia with her beloved family and many pets. She is a minister with a BA degree from Old Dominion University who loves to garden, cook, read, sculpt, and intentionally practice being The New Beatitudes. She is thrilled to share this profound teaching and looks forward to hearing from the readers about their experiences and resulting miracles and enlightenment.

You may contact Keith at www.spiritualityforthecommonman.com. She deeply desires to inspire mankind to *be love, be forgiveness, be One, be respectful all life, be joy, be gratitude, be peace, be present,* and *be* The New Beatitudes, so as to uplift and change the world for the better now.

Appendix

1. Day, Sharon Pieroni, *The Book, The Creator's Template for Eternal Life*, Create Space, Charleston, S.C., 2010.
2. *A Course in Miracles*, Foundation for Inner Peace, 1975, 1985, 1992.
3. *The Holy Bible*, King James Version, Matthew, Exodus, New World Publishing.
4. Hanna, Linda Schiller, Channelled unpublished material, 2014.
5. Coates, Judith, *Jeshua The Personal Christ*, Volume II, Oakbridge University Press, 1996.

Made in the USA
Middletown, DE
27 September 2019